CU00820047

Corporate Governanc

Corporate Governance Unlocked

Alison Dillon Kibirige
and Winifred Tarinyeba Kiryabwire

The Governance
Institute

First published 2019

Published by
ICSA Publishing Ltd
Saffron House, 6–10 Kirby Street
London EC1N 8TS

© ICSA Publishing Ltd, 2019

Typeset by Paul Barrett Book Production, Cambridge
Printed in Great Britain by Lightning Source, Milton Keynes, Buckinghamshire

British Cataloguing in Publication Data
A catalogue record for this book is available from the British Library.

ISBN 978-1-86072-721-4

Contents

Acronyms and abbreviations

ABI	Association of British Insurers
ACCA	Association of Chartered Certified Accountants
AGM	Annual General Meeting
APRM	African Peer Review Mechanism
CACG	Commonwealth Association for Corporate Governance
CalPERS	California Public Employees Retirement System
CEO	Chief Executive Officer
CFO	Chief Financial Officer
CSIA	Corporate Secretaries International Association
CSR	Corporate Social Responsibility
DFID	Department of International Development
ECGI	European Corporate Governance Institute
EPA	Environmental Protection Agency
ESG	Environment, Social and Governance
EU	European Union
EWCA	England & Wales Court of Appeal
FCA	Financial Conduct Authority
FRC	Financial Reporting Council
FSB	Financial Stability Board
FTSE	Financial Times Stock Exchange
GE	General Electric
GRI	Global Reporting Initiative
HSBC	Hong Kong and Shanghai Banking Corporation
ICGN	International Corporate Governance Network
ICSA	Institute of Chartered Secretaries and Administrators
IFAC	International Federation of Accountants
IFC	International Finance Corporation
IIA	Institute of Internal Auditors
IIRC	International Integrated Reporting Council
IMA	Investment Management Authority
IOD	Institute of Directors

IOSCO	International Organisation of Securities Commissions
IPO	Initial Public Offering
IRM	Institute of Risk Management
ISS	Institute Shareholders Services
IVIS	Institutional Voting Information Service
KPMG	Klynueld Peat Marwick Goerdeler
LIBOR	London Inter-bank Offered Rate
MSC	Marine Stewardship Council
NAPF	National Association of Pension Funds
NEPAD	New Partnership for Africa's Development
NGOs	Non Government Organisations
NYSE	New York Stock Exchange
OECD	Organisation for Economic Co-operation and Development
PCH II	Polygon Credit Holdings II Limited
PRA	Prudential Regulatory Authority
PRI	Principles for Responsible Investment
RDS	Royal Dutch Shell
REACH	Directive on Registration, Evaluation and Authorization of Chemicals
RoHS	Restriction of Hazardous Substance Directive
S&P	Standard and Poor companies
SMEs	Small and Medium Enterprises
TFG	Tetragon Financial Group
TSR	Total Shareholder Return
UKRIAT	UK, Republic of Ireland and Associated Territories
UN	United Nations
VW	Volkswagen
WEEE	Waste Electrical and Electronic Equipment Directive
WWF	World Wildlife Fund

Introduction

Corporate governance is a commonly used term. It is, however, often misunderstood and confused with compliance. Many organisations implement corporate governance best practices without truly embedding the practices and developing the cultures that those best practices were designed to create. This has led in some cases to the many corporate governance scandals that we have all read and heard about.

The aim of this book is to broaden your understanding of what corporate governance is, and how and why it has developed in the way it has, and give you some pointers on how best practice is applied in all different types of organisations in the private, public and not-for-profit sectors.

The book focuses on how the three main corporate governance regimes internationally form the basis of corporate governance best practice. These are:

- the UK Corporate Governance framework;
- the G20/OECD Corporate Governance Principles; and
- the King Reports from South Africa.

The book does not cover corporate governance in the USA, which has developed its own specific corporate governance requirements.

The authors of the book work internationally and are not UK based. Their perspectives illustrate global understanding of best practice in corporate governance, which may in some circumstances be different from the UK perspective. It is hoped that the introduction of these different perspectives will enrich discussion of the topic.

Chapter 1 looks at definitions, concepts, approaches and elements of corporate governance. It also discusses whether countries should regulate corporate governance practices or leave them to be applied by organisations in a voluntary manner.

Chapter 2 deals with the governance framework for organisations and explains both internal and external governance frameworks. Both constitute the overall governance architecture for organisations. Internal governance frameworks include the Articles of Association or constitution, shareholder agreements and internal policies. External governance frameworks vary depending on the nature of organisation and include laws such as company law, or other organisational laws such as trust law or laws governing the establishment of not-for-profit organisations, other legal and regulatory frameworks such as securities laws and laws governing regulated entities such as banks, insurance companies and pension funds among others. Corporate governance codes are also part of the external governance frameworks.

Chapter 3 describes the evolution of corporate governance from its origins in the UK, and how it has developed as a discipline, internationally across the globe, sector by sector and also by organisational type.

Chapter 4 seeks to explain the roles of all the governance players within an organisation: shareholders, board, management and company secretary.

Chapter 5 looks at the role of professionals – accountants, lawyers and compliance officers – and of the representative bodies that are involved in corporate governance. It also considers the impact of regulators and shareholder representative bodies on an organisation's corporate governance practices.

Chapter 6 explains the rationale and value of stakeholder engagement. There is a growing awareness within organisations that it is important for the success of the organisation that the interests of stakeholders are taken into consideration when making decisions.

Chapter 7 describes what is meant by corporate social responsibility (CSR) and what drives organisations to be more socially responsible. It also considers how CSR can be integrated into an organisation's strategy to achieve long-term sustainability for the organisation. The chapter finally looks at how organisations are reporting on their CSR activities.

Chapter 8 explains the link between governance and ethics, and discusses how organisations can create an ethical culture. There is a tendency to think that legal, regulatory and other responses to governance failures including criminal and civil prosecution of the culprits will deter wrongdoing. History has shown that this is not the case and has taught us that ethics is central to governance.

Chapter 9 considers future trends in corporate governance. It explores how corporate governance practices are being used to resolve some global common issues, such as executive pay, increased regulation, the impact of the millennial generation and the societal impact of organisational activities.

1 Introduction to corporate governance

Introduction

This chapter looks at definitions, concepts, approaches and elements of corporate governance. It also discusses whether countries should regulate corporate governance practices or leave them to be applied by organisations in a voluntary manner.

Corporate governance defined

Corporate governance is a misunderstood and often misused term. It was first used in a code to describe a series of best practices suggested for listed companies to protect investors in the UK. These best practices had been created to deal with a series of high-profile corporate collapses in the UK in the late 1980s and early 1990s, most notably Polly Peck International (1990), the Bank of Credit and Commerce International (1991), the Mirror Group News International (1991) and Barings Bank (1995). Corporate scandals in other parts of the globe, such as Enron (2001) in the USA, have led to other countries adopting corporate governance best practices to protect their investors. Since 2000, further corporate collapses and the global financial crisis have led to corporate governance best practices being expanded to deal with other stakeholder issues, among them pension protection, climate change, scarcity of natural resources, community issues and ethical malpractices.

Corporate governance best practices have also spread in many countries to non-listed companies and other organisations across all three sectors: private, public and not-for-profit.

Since no two organisations are the same, there is no 'one size fits all' corporate governance solution. Organisations, therefore, have to consider which best practices to adopt to help their organisations to develop sustainably and create better performance and increased value. This requires organisations to have the capacity to recognise which practices should be adopted at what stage of an organisation's development. This has been lacking and has led to either an avoidance of corporate governance best practices or the bland adoption of inappropriate practices. It has also led to a belief by many entrepreneurs and senior executives that corporate governance is costly, bureaucratic and something to be avoided.

In many parts of the world, corporate governance has become synonymous with compliance. Many companies (as was evidenced by the 2008 global financial crisis) still see corporate governance as a mere box-ticking exercise against laws, regulations, standards and codes rather than an important tool which, if truly embraced, can lead to better-performing and more sustainable organisations.

Many companies still see complying with the letter and not the spirit of laws, regulations, standards and codes as sufficient as seen in the 'tax avoidance' cases, such as Starbucks (see case study below), Apple, Google and Amazon. In the Starbucks case, the company actually issued a statement which said that they had done nothing illegal. They had complied with the law. This response created a backlash from the general public who seemed to care not whether what the company did was right or wrong in terms of the law but whether it was right or wrong morally. Simply complying with regulations, standards and codes seems to create reputational risk; the management of this, as we will see later in the chapter, is a key concept of corporate governance. Organisations should see governance as 'doing the right thing' which may take them above the letter of the law but that, after all, is a minimum standard.

The evolution of corporate governance will be discussed in more detail in Chapter 2. It has, however, led to confusion about the term and how and when it should be applied.

CASE STUDY: STARBUCKS

In 2012, Starbucks, known for its strong corporate responsibility and customer service, came under scrutiny for its UK tax payments. In the previous year, 2011, despite making sales of £398 million, Starbucks paid no corporation tax. The company showed a loss in its annual financial statements of £32.9 million due to a charge of £107.2 million of 'administrative expenses' which appeared to represent, in part, royalty fees for UK division franchises.

In a statement, Starbucks insisted that it had 'paid and will continue to pay its fair share of taxes in full compliance with all UK tax laws, as it always has'. It went on to say that Starbucks was considered to be a good tax-payer by UK regulators and behaved in a moral way, balancing profit with social conscience.

The UK public was outraged by Starbucks' comments and started to boycott and protest outside the company's coffee shops. Starbucks' response was to offer to pay, over a period of years, £20 million in corporation tax despite its continued loss making, 'to please its customers'. In a statement, the company said, 'We felt that our customers should not have to wait for us to become profitable before we started paying UK corporation tax.' Source – *The Week* (June 2013)

What is corporate governance?

'Governance' refers to the way in which something is governed and to the function of governing. All organisations, therefore, practise governance. The question should be how well they practise it – if they do this well, their organisation should survive and flourish.

The term governance was first associated with corporations in 1984 when coined by Bob Tricker. The term was picked up by Sir Adrian Cadbury for the 'Report of the Committee on Financial Aspects of Corporate Governance' (the Cadbury Report) which was published in the UK in 1992. The Cadbury Committee was set up to identify how investors could be protected against the bad practices of the managers of listed companies.

Since 1992, the term corporate governance has gained a great deal of prominence, with most countries around the world adopting some measure of corporate governance best practices. However, if you gather together a group of people interested in corporate governance, there will be significant differences in how they define what corporate governance is, and in some cases disagreement about what corporate governance seeks to achieve and how this should be achieved. This is due to the differences in the types of organisations, markets, economies and issues that the best practices are being introduced to deal with.

There is, therefore, no one definition of corporate governance. Every document referring to corporate governance seems to use its own definition.

This probably reflects the earlier statement that all organisations are different, so 'no one size fits all'.

Some of the more well-known definitions are as follows.

The system by which companies are directed and controlled. This definition is from the 'Report of the Committee on Financial Aspects of Corporate Governance' (the Cadbury Report). The Report included a Code of Best Practice (the Cadbury Code), which applied to all companies listed on the London Stock Exchange. This was the first corporate governance code of best practice.

> Involves a set of relationships between a company's management, its Board, its shareholders and other stakeholders ... also provides the structure through which the objectives of the company are set, and the means of attaining those objectives and monitoring performance are determined.

This definition is from the Organisation for Economic Co-operation and Development's (OECD) Principles of Corporate Governance, issued in 1999 and reviewed and amended in 2004 and 2015. In 2015, these Principles became known as the G20/OECD Corporate Governance Principles when they were endorsed by the G20 leaders. The revised Principles stated that the purpose of corporate governance is 'to help build an environment of trust transparency and accountability necessary for fostering long-term investment, financial stability and business integrity, thereby supporting stronger growth and more inclusive societies'.

The Principles are intended to serve as a reference point for countries when they are evaluating their legal, institutional and regulatory provisions for corporate governance. They also offer guidance and suggestions for stock exchanges, investors, companies and other bodies involved in developing good corporate governance practices.

> The exercise of ethical and effective leadership by the governing body towards the achievement of the following governance outcomes:
> - Ethical culture
> - Good performance
> - Effective control
> - Legitimacy

This definition comes from King IV (2016) which was developed in South Africa by the Institute of Directors to cater for the specific governance issues facing organisations in South Africa. The definition brings into corporate governance the concepts of corporate citizenship (ethics and corporate responsibility) and also of organisation sustainability.

The UK Corporate Governance Code 2016 stated that 'the purpose of corporate governance is to facilitate effective, entrepreneurial and prudent management that can deliver the long-term success of the company'. It refers back to the definition of corporate governance from the Cadbury Report, and states that the 2016 Code is still set within the context of this definition: 'corporate governance is therefore about what the board of a company does and how it sets the values of the company. It is to be distinguished from the day to day operational management of the company by full-time executives.' The 2018 UK Corporate Governance Code expands the definition, recognising that companies do not exist in isolation: 'To succeed in the long-term, directors and the companies they lead need to build and maintain successful relationships with a wide range of stakeholders.'

The African Peer Review Mechanism (APRM) defines organisations as conducting good corporate governance if they are seen to pursue eight distinguishing characteristics: discipline, transparency, independence, accountability, responsibility, fairness, ethical conduct and good corporate citizenship. These traits are believed to be important because evidence shows that they lead to better-performing organisations which are sustainable in the long term. This results in economic development as these organisations contribute more to the economy and to society as a whole directly through the wages and taxes they pay, and indirectly through the money they pay their supply chain, the vendors, retail outlets, service and training firms, and resellers of their products and services.

Should it matter that there is not one definition of corporate governance?

We will see in the next chapter when we look at the development of corporate governance that the lack of a clear definition has resulted in a plethora of corporate governance regulations around the world. These have mainly been reacting to a particular circumstance and some, though well intended, have been poorly conceived. Each initiative has tended to add to the compliance burden of organisations, especially companies listed on a stock exchange. This presents a problem in many countries where companies, some of which are not listed, are encouraged to comply

ιappropriate international governance standards as a means
investors.

Many organisations that could benefit from some aspects of corporate
governance best practice also dismiss it as not being applicable to them
because they are not corporate. For example, much of the service and
product delivery in developing countries is by organisations in the public
and not-for-profit sectors, many of which are not accountable for or
transparent about their activities. Non-corporates therefore lose out on
the benefits of adopting good governance practices, such as sustainability,
cheaper capital, less risk, etc. For organisations in developing countries,
this is particularly important since for sustainable economic development,
organisations across all three sectors (private, public and not-for-profit)
are needed. Corporate governance in the non-listed private sector is also
in its infancy and needs to develop to produce the much-needed engine
for growth. The UK is considering introducing a new code for larger
private companies.

Corporate governance practitioners within developing countries are
therefore undertaking initiatives to reposition corporate governance in
the region as a method of achieving organisational sustainability and
growth in addition to the traditional view of attracting capital through
protection of investors. The introduction of good corporate governance
practices within an organisation should therefore always be aimed at
providing long-term benefits in terms of sustainability and growth to an
organisation that substantially exceed the cost of their implementation.
Organisations should consider, as part of their strategic planning, how
they can make their business more sustainable and profitable in the long
term through introducing these practices. Organisations in developed
countries should arguably also be taking the same approach.

The plethora of laws, regulations, standards and codes around the
topic of corporate governance are intended to help organisations identify
best practices which should improve their governance. Deciding 'what'
best practices should be adopted and 'why' is, however, only part of the
governance equation. Practitioners in governance have realised that 'how'
these best practices are implemented and maintained effectively in an
organisation creates true governance and the benefits which are
associated with it.

Figure 1.1 explains why. True governance revolves around how people
in the organisation operationalise the infrastructure of structures, policies

and procedures which have been put in place. If the infrastructure is appropriate for the organisation, people are focused and work well together, resources are used effectively and information flows smoothly. Decisions are then made effectively, and this all contributes to a successful sustainable organisation. If the infrastructure is not appropriate for the organisation then the anticipated 'cultures' will not be developed. Those within the organisation will develop their own cultures which, as they are not being managed, often leads to bad practices, such as failure to follow policies, the misuse of resources, breakdown of important relationships, etc. This in turn threatens the performance and long-term sustainability of the organisation.

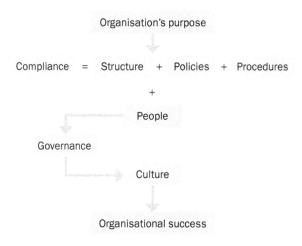

Figure 1.1: Compliance vs Governance

Concepts of corporate governance

Despite there being no agreed definition of corporate governance, there are several agreed concepts underlying the development of corporate governance. These concepts can be found operating to different degrees in all types of organisations whichever sector they are in: private, public or not-for-profit. These concepts are:

- accountability;
- responsibility;
- transparency; and
- fairness.

Accountability

This refers to the requirement for a person or group of people in a position of responsibility to account for the exercise (or not) of the authority they have been given. Accountability should be to the person or group of people from whom the authority is derived.

Those providing accountability should provide 'honest' information and not manipulate facts or 'spin' them to their or their organisation's advantage.

Accountability applies to all the different 'players' within an organisation, whether they are the owners of the organisation, the governing body, the management or the employees. The challenge is in deciding how the person or group of people should be made accountable, and over what time period.

Corporate governance best practice requires an organisation to set out clearly who is accountable for what and over what time period so that an organisation's stakeholders are clear whom they should hold responsible for what. The sophistication of how this is set out will again depend on the size and complexity of the organisation, and can range from a few lines to a large manual as the organisation becomes more complex.

Responsibility

This refers to a person or group of people having authority over something, and who are, therefore, liable to be held accountable for the exercise or lack of exercise of that authority. Those given authorities should accept full responsibility for the powers that they have been given and the authority they exercise. They should understand what their responsibilities are, and should carry them out ethically with honesty, probity and integrity.

Organisations should ensure that procedures and structures are in place so that people know what they are responsible for and thus liable to account for. This will help people to minimise, or avoid completely, potential conflicts of interest that could arise in the exercise or lack of exercise of their authority. Mismanagement of authority should be penalised, and therefore responsibility goes hand in hand with accountability.

Transparency

This refers to the ease with which an outsider is able to make a meaningful analysis of an organisation and its actions, both financial and non-financial. It also refers to the clarity of process in making decisions and carrying them out. Transparency builds trust between the organisation and its stakeholders: those with whom it interacts or who have an interest in the organisation.

Organisations should:

- be open in all of their actions, relationships, processes and decision-making. This includes tenders, recruitment and disclosures about business performance and risks; and
- ensure that disclosure is timely and accurate on all material matters, including: the financial situation, performance, ownership and corporate governance. It does not include commercially sensitive information, for example, The Coca-Cola Company would not be required to disclose the recipe for the Coca-Cola drink.

Those interested in the organisation need to know about it in order to make informed decisions when dealing with it. Information disclosure needs to be timely to be of benefit to its recipients. It can be delivered through press releases, market releases and an organisation's website.

Organisations should have policies in place about the disclosure of information – what information should be public and what information should be kept secret, who has authority to disclose what information and when, etc. They should also have a policy and process on how information should be kept confidential once it has been classified as confidential information.

Fairness

This refers to the principle that all key stakeholders should be treated fairly when decisions are made or actions taken by the organisation. The organisation should provide effective redress for violations, for example, to minority shareholders when they have been unfairly treated.

Again, organisations should have policies, structures and procedures in place to ensure that the organisation and the people within consider key stakeholder views with justice and avoidance of bias or vested interests. Fair practices should be applied in an organisations dealings with stakeholders. These dealings should also adhere to the spirit, not just the letter, of all rules and regulations that govern the organisation. An example of this would be where an organisation outsources to lower cost suppliers in emerging or developing markets who achieve the lower costs through less favourable working practices such as sweat shops and child labour. The organisation hopes to benefit through higher profits and the senior executives through higher bonuses.

Reputational management

In addition to the above concepts, many corporate governance experts now see reputational management as an important issue within corporate governance. Reputation defines an organisation as well as the individuals associated with that organisation. A good reputation attracts and motivates employees, customers and investors, and also assists in raising cash. The destruction of a reputation can lead to the end of the organisation. For example, the global accounting firm Arthur Andersen was destroyed by the damage of its involvement in the Enron affair in the USA.

Organisations must, therefore, have structures and processes in place to manage reputational risk. Judy Larkin (2002) identified the benefits of effective reputational management, which can be summarised as follows:

- improving relations with shareholders;
- creating a more favourable environment for investment and access to capital;
- recruiting and retaining the best employees;
- attracting the best business partners, suppliers and customers;
- reducing barriers to development in new markets;
- securing premium prices for products and/or services;
- minimising threats of litigation and of more stringent regulation;
- reducing the potential for crises; and
- reinforcing the organisation's credibility and trust for stakeholders.

Approaches to corporate governance

In addition to agreed concepts of corporate governance, experts also agree on three main approaches to corporate governance. These are:

- shareholder value approach;
- stakeholder approach; and
- inclusive stakeholder approach.

Shareholder value approach

The shareholder value approach to corporate governance states that the board of directors should govern their company in the best interests of its owners, the shareholders. The main objective is to maximise the wealth of a company's shareholders through share price growth and dividend payments, while conforming to the rules of society as embedded in laws and customs. The directors should only be accountable to the shareholders, who should have the power to appoint them and remove them from office if their performance is inadequate. This approach therefore also focuses on protecting investors and the value of their shareholding in the company.

Enlightened shareholder value approach

An 'enlightened' shareholder value approach has been adopted in some advanced economies, for example the UK. This approach proposes that boards, when considering actions to maximise shareholder value, should look to the long term as well as the short term, and consider the views of and impact on other stakeholders in the company, not just shareholders. The views of stakeholders are, however, only considered in so far as it would be in the interests of shareholders to do so.

Non-corporates can also adopt an investor value approach to their governance. Investors in not-for-profit and public sector organisations can expect a 'social impact' as value for their investment. For example, in developing economies an investor in private sector agribusiness will expect value for money from the activities undertaken by the organisations in which they invest.

Stakeholder approach

The stakeholder or pluralist approach to corporate governance states that companies should have regard to the views of all stakeholders, not just shareholders. This would include the public at large. When taking decisions, boards of companies should try to balance the interests of all the company's stakeholders.

The stakeholder approach to corporate governance is predominantly adopted in civil law countries, such as France and Germany, and in Japan and China where companies are often required to take account of the social and financial interests of employees, creditors and consumers in their decision making.

Opponents of the stakeholder approach argue that if companies were to take into account all stakeholders' conflicting views, they would never come to a decision. However, there is no direct evidence that one approach is superior to the other in terms of the success of the organisation. The growing body of evidence seems to imply it is the adoption of good governance practices that is important for the sustainability and success of an organisation.

Inclusive stakeholder approach

This approach is contained in the New Partnership for Africa's Development (NEPAD) definition of corporate governance and also in the South African King Reports, developed by the Institute of Directors in South Africa. The approach differs in its emphasis from the enlightened shareholder approach in that its supporters believe that the board of directors should consider the legitimate interests and expectations of key stakeholders on the basis that this is in the best interests of the company. The legitimate interests and expectations of key stakeholders should be included in the board's decision-making process and traded off against each other on a case-by-case basis in the best interests of the company.

There is, therefore, a subtle difference between this approach and the enlightened shareholder approach. In the inclusive approach, the shareholder does not have any predetermined precedence over other stakeholders. The best interests of the company are defined by the Institute of Directors for Southern Africa, King Code of Governance for South Africa 2009, King III, not in terms of maximising shareholder value, but 'within the parameters of the company as a sustainable enterprise and the company as a corporate citizen'. This definition has been carried into the latest edition of the King Codes King IV.

The 'stakeholder inclusive' approach reflects African needs and culture. It incorporates the concepts of sustainability and 'good citizenship' (incorporating ethics and corporate social responsibility) as part of the fight against corruption and HIV/AIDS, and the aim to eradicate poverty through economic development. These concepts are often seen in the shareholder value approach as complementary disciplines.

Benefits and disadvantages of the different approaches to corporate governance

Supporters of each of the approaches often passionately cite benefits of the approach they support, and the disadvantages of other approaches. Johnson *et al.* (2008) outlined the main differences between the approaches, which are presented in Table 1.1.

Table 1.1: Benefits and disadvantages of governance approaches

	Shareholder model	Stakeholder model
Benefits	For investors: • high rate of return • reduced risk. For the economy: • encourages entrepreneurship • encourages inward investment. For management: • independence.	For investors: • closer monitoring of management • longer-term decision horizons. For stakeholders: • deterrent to high-risk decisions.
Disadvantages	For investors: • difficult to monitor management. For the economy: • risk of short-termism and top management greed.	For management: • potential interference • slower decision making • reduced independence. For the economy: • reduced financing opportunities for growth.

Convergence of approaches

Proponents of each approach to governance have traditionally been very protective of their approach, seeing the shareholder value and stakeholder approaches as being diametrically opposed. Table 1.1 reflects this approach.

However, trends today seem to support convergence of the two main approaches to corporate governance: the shareholder value approach and the stakeholder approach. As we saw above in Africa where many countries follow the common law system, 'in the best interests of the company 'is being redefined as 'the long-term sustainability of the company', which appears to resemble more closely the stakeholder approach, rather than being 'in the best interests of shareholders'. This is not seen as at odds with being in the shareholders' best interests.

In civil law countries, pressure is being exerted to give priority to the interests of shareholders. For example, in France, the Marini Report criticised the concept of company interest, since it brought the danger of having management act primarily in its own interests. In Japan, corporate governance principles suggest on the one hand that a balance of various interests must be drawn, but on the other hand that the providers of capital are at the core of corporate governance.

Whichever approach to corporate governance is adopted, one of the underlying issues corporate governance attempts to deal with is conflicts of interest (potential or actual) between shareholders, members of the board as a whole or as individual members, and stakeholders. Directors may be tempted to take risks for short-term benefit whereas shareholders and many stakeholders will be looking to the long term. If a company gets into financial difficulty, directors can usually move on to another company with limited or no financial loss, leaving the shareholders and other stakeholders to suffer the fallout and loss.

Best practices in corporate governance

Best practices in corporate governance tend to fall into five areas. You would expect to see these appropriately reflected in organisations that are committed to good corporate governance. These are:

- good board practices;
- controlled environment;
- transparent disclosure;
- good corporate citizenship; and
- effective relationship with stakeholders.

Good board practices

These are evidenced by a well-structured board with the appropriate composition and mix of skills. Members of the board have clearly defined roles and authorities, and understand their duties and responsibilities. The appropriate procedures are in place to ensure that the board performs efficiently. A board evaluation is carried to ensure that the members of the board are up to date and have all the relevant information to enable them to make informed decisions. The board discusses corporate governance issues regularly and commits appropriate resources to them. Remuneration for the board is in line with best practice. Finally, operation of the board by way of board committees enhances its performance.

Controlled environment

A risk management framework enables the organisation to identify, assess and mitigate risks. If appropriate for the size of the organisation, an independent audit committee is established. Internal control procedures are also introduced together with management information systems which check whether the internal control procedures are effective. Again. if appropriate for the size and type of organisation, an internal auditor, audit function and/or compliance function are established to ensure that policies and procedures are appropriate and complied with. If the organisation requires audited financial statements to be published, then the external auditor will have to be independent.

Transparent disclosure

The organisation discloses both financial and non-financial information to its stakeholders, including its shareholders, on a timely basis. Financial statements are prepared according to international financial requirements or, if more appropriate to the organisation, local financial reporting standards. Financial statements are audited by an independent external auditor. Information that is disclosed is of a high quality and is released through all appropriate mediums, e.g. press releases, annual reports, websites.

Organisations are also transparent in all their processes, transactions and decision making; for example, recruitment, procurement, business performance and risks.

Good corporate citizenship

The organisation has well-defined stakeholder policies. Policies are written on major areas of concern for stakeholders such as corporate social responsibility and environmental issues. Organisations report using integrated or 'triple bottom line' reporting, which concentrates on the social, environmental and economic impact of their activities on the communities where they operate. The impact reported should be positive; where it is negative, organisations explain how they are going to eradicate or reduce the negative impact. The organisation has a code of ethics based on the ethical values of the organisation.

Effective relationship with stakeholders

The organisation identifies key stakeholders (which includes, for companies, its shareholders) and their legitimate interests and expectations. Constructive dialogue occurs with key stakeholders to balance the interests of the organisation with those legitimate interests and expectations of key stakeholders in the long term. The organisation ensures that processes are in place to ensure that all shareholders are treated equally and that the rights of minority shareholders are respected.

Should countries regulate corporate governance?

As mentioned above, corporate governance is an international concern. Different countries have adopted and implemented corporate governance practices to varying degrees and in different ways.

Principles-based approach

As we shall see in the next chapter, current international best practices in corporate governance were developed in the UK in the 1990s with codes of best practice such as the Cadbury Code 1992. Other countries followed suit and adopted their own codes of best practice. These codes, which were developed for listed companies to protect investors, adopted a 'comply or explain' approach, discussed later in the chapter. Listed companies are required to comply with the provisions of the code or explain to their shareholders why they have not complied. These companies have shareholders and shareholder representative bodies, who can assess whether the explanation is acceptable or not.

This approach to corporate governance is called the principles-based approach and allows companies and their shareholders to choose to adopt the provisions of the code or explain why they believe it is not appropriate to do so. It was hoped that the introduction of codes based on 'principles' would restrict the regulatory burden on companies. The approach recognises the need for flexibility due to the diversity of circumstances and experiences within companies, and the fact that non-compliance may, at that time in a company's life cycle, be in the organisation's best interests. Principles-based codes still exist today in the UK and in many other countries.

Some countries, such as the UK, have adopted principles-based codes of practice for institutional shareholders. The aim is to encourage institutional shareholders to take a more active role in the governance of those companies in which they invest. It is argued that institutional shareholders, such as pension funds, unit trusts and life assurance companies, hold funds on behalf of many individuals and are therefore investing indirectly on behalf of those individuals. They thus have a responsibility on behalf of those individuals to make sure that the boards of directors of the companies in which they invest are made properly accountable and govern their companies responsibly.

Many business leaders say a principles-based approach, allowing for discretion based on the circumstances of the company, is far preferable to a rigid rules-based approach. They claim that evidence suggests that long-term economic development is best achieved when business leaders are permitted to exercise judgement. However, the catalogue of business scandals over the last 20 years seems to indicate that some sort of regulation may be needed to ensure that good governance prevails in businesses, and stakeholders and stakeholder interests are protected.

Even in the UK, questions are being asked as to whether current market structures which are very different from those in place in the early 1990s are still able to regulate listed companies in the way envisaged. In 1992, over 50% of the shares of companies listed on the London Stock Exchange were owned by UK pension funds and insurance companies. In 2014, according to the UK Office of National Statistics, this figure had dropped to less than 10%. In addition, it would appear that the UK equity market is less important to UK investors than it used to be. According to the Pensions and Lifetime Saving's Association, between 2005 and 2012, the percentage of assets that defined benefit pension schemes allocated to UK equities fell from 32% to 10%. This trend was also reflected in a 2016 survey on asset management by the UK's Investment Association, which showed that only 13% of its members' assets under management were invested in UK equities, down from over 25% in 2007. The concern is that with limited resources and time UK investors are going to be devoting their energies to monitoring the corporate governance performance of UK listed companies. Evidence has also shown that in addition to time and resource, overseas investors face practical barriers to direct engagement with UK companies. Neither of these developments bode well for a future self-regulating system for the UK market.

Rules-based or mandatory approach

Following several well-publicised scandals in the USA, including Enron (2001), WorldCom (2002) and Tyco (2002), the country decided to adopt an alternative approach to corporate governance. In the Sarbanes Oxley Act 2002, the USA legislated to protect investors by adopting a mandatory rules-based approach to corporate governance. Companies have to comply with the provisions of the Act. However, the question is: 'How do countries introduce regulation without affecting their long-term economic development?'

Regulation, it is argued, only works where the challenges faced by companies under the purview of the regulation are substantially similar, justifying a common approach to common problems and if the rules and their enforcement efficiently and effectively direct, modify or preclude the behaviours they are aimed at affecting.

The debate continues around the world as to whether a rules-based approach or a principles-based approach is best. Whichever route is taken, corporate governance should be flexible enough to allow business leaders to make decisions that are in the best interests of their firms, for sustainability. The adoption of best practices should be appropriate to the company's stage of development.

Hybrid approach

Many developing countries struggle with the issue of how to encourage the adoption of good corporate governance practices without stifling economic growth. The issue is made worse by the fact that very few companies are listed on stock exchanges. The media is often expected to fill this gap by reporting on good and bad practices of corporate governance. The reality is that many journalists are ill equipped to fill this role.

This makes governments and regulators nervous about leaving important decisions about how businesses are governed to those running them. They therefore feel obligated to regulate to protect shareholders and other stakeholders. Hybrid systems have emerged where some corporate governance provisions are found in legislation and others in codes of best practice.

'Comply or explain' or 'apply and explain'

The first corporate governance code in the UK, the 'Report of the Committee on the Financial Aspects of Corporate Governance: The Code of Best Practice' (Cadbury Code), required companies listed on the London Stock Exchange to 'comply or explain' with the provisions of the Code. It was argued by many that this led to a box-ticking approach by investors and companies. Investors judged a company on whether it had complied or not with the provisions without considering the reasons and appropriateness of not complying. Companies also tried to comply with the provisions, even when they were inappropriate, fearing that non-compliance might bring disfavour from investors with the accompanying adverse reputational impact.

King IV has adopted the 'apply and explain' approach which was first adopted in King III. The introduction to King III explains that the 'apply or explain' approach 'shows an appreciation for the fact that it is often not a case of whether to comply or not, but rather to consider how the principles and recommendations can be applied'. This approach is helpful in markets where corporate governance is in its infancy and applies to all organisations, not just listed companies. Organisations can show a progression in their application of good corporate governance practices over time.

Corporate governance in developing countries

In developing countries, good corporate governance can make it easier for organisations to raise capital and finance investment. Banks and investors have more confidence in organisations with good governance. It is hoped that improved corporate governance in all forms of organisations, especially when done in the context of wider economic and systemic governance, will enhance the confidence of financial institutions and investors, both domestic and foreign. If a country is seen to have weak corporate governance practices generally, then that country will struggle to attract foreign investment. Countries too need foreign investment for their economies to grow. If countries, especially developing countries, are to succeed in attracting inward capital investment through international capital markets, their corporate governance practices need to be understood by and acceptable to the international investment community.

Within many developing countries, good corporate governance is applied to all forms of organisations, as many organisations in the public and not-for-profit sectors are the main service delivery vehicles. To apply the concepts of good governance to just the private sector would therefore not bring the widespread improvement required.

Economies in developing countries rely on businesses, such as agriculture, mining and other extractive industries that have adverse effects on the environment. Organisations should conduct their operations in a way that meets existing needs without compromising the ability of future generations to meet their needs. This means having regard to the impact that the organisation's operations have on the environmental, economic and social life of the community in which it operates. In addition, abject poverty, hunger and often health issues such as HIV/ AIDS, malaria, diabetes and tuberculosis afflict many communities. As well as being an economic entity, an organisation is a citizen of its country of operation and as such has a moral and social standing within that society, with all the responsibilities attached to that status. It should act as society would expect of any good citizen.

Chapter summary

- There are no agreed definitions or approaches to corporate governance.
- When companies collapse, poor corporate governance is often to blame.
- Adopting good governance practices results in sustainability and good performance over the longer term.
- There is agreement on four concepts of corporate governance: accountability, responsibility, transparency and fairness. However, the interpretation of these four words can differ.

- There is a growing recognition that reputational risk and the protection of an organisation's reputation are also of growing importance when discussing corporate governance.
- Countries adopt corporate governance in different ways through laws, regulations, standards and codes of best practice.

2   The governance framework

Introduction

This chapter deals with the governance framework for organisations and explains both internal and external governance frameworks. Both constitute the overall governance architecture for organisations. Internal governance frameworks include the Articles of Association/constitution, shareholder agreements and internal policies. External governance frameworks vary depending on the nature of organisation and include laws, regulations and other standards with which organisations are required to comply.

What is a governance framework?

When we talk about corporate governance, we tend to think about the board of an organisation or key corporate governance principles, such as accountability, transparency or fairness. It is true that the board or governing body of an organisation is the custodian of corporate governance; however, governance is much broader than the board or the key governance principles. So what is a governance framework? Before we answer this question, it might be useful to draw an analogy from governments. Constitutionally, there are three arms of government: the executive, the judiciary and the legislature. All three contribute to the overall governance of a country and have roles and responsibilities that are clearly outlined in the constitution or equivalent law of the country. Similarly, organisations have governance frameworks that comprise various components or organs, each with clear roles and responsibilities. Governance frameworks may vary depending on the nature or type of organisation.

In the public sector, there are different types of organisations such as district councils or regulatory bodies (such as the Bank of England, the Financial Conduct Authority and the Charities Commission). These are usually established by law and have their governance frameworks prescribed by the law that established them. In the private sector, there are various types of organisations that include private companies, listed companies, charities, associations and trusts among others. Their governance frameworks vary and they have different objectives.

Governance frameworks comprise internal and external frameworks. Both contribute to the overall governance of an organisation. Internal frameworks are largely determined by the parties and include the charter/constitution/Articles of Association as well as ethics codes and policies that guide the daily operations of the organisation. External frameworks vary and may be mandatory or voluntary depending on the nature of the organisation. Figure 2.1 provides an overview of internal and external governance frameworks.

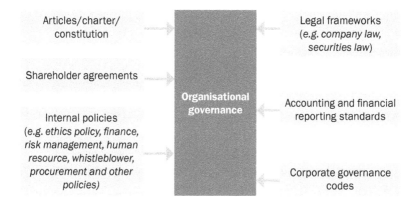

Figure 2.1: An illustration of internal and external governance frameworks

Governance frameworks are important and can lead to governance failures if there are weaknesses within the framework, such as lack of clarity of roles, weak oversight and accountability mechanisms or concentration of power without adequate checks. Governance frameworks may vary but for every organisation, they provide the foundation for corporate governance. Therefore, things like the purpose and objectives of an organisation, and the roles and responsibilities of the governing bodies (which are often set out in foundation documents such as the Memorandum and Articles of Association or constitution or charter), are important aspects of the governance framework.

External governance frameworks such as company law and other organisational laws such as securities laws provide the benchmark for standards and conduct and regulation of relationships of various parties such as owners, managers, creditors and investors.

Governance frameworks assist governing bodies such as boards of directors to establish and execute their governance responsibilities. They also provide a framework for assessing governance risks. An organisation is able to determine whether the framework is adequate or whether governance arrangements are aligned with the existing framework.

It is important to understand that a governance framework is not cast in stone. As organisations grow and transform, and as changes or threats emerge, it is important to review frameworks and ensure that governance arrangements and governance frameworks are adequate or fit for purpose. For example, the 2001 corporate failures in the United States and the 2008 financial crisis revealed weaknesses that needed to be addressed to improve governance including structure and composition of boards, independence of the audit function, risk management and governance of ethics. In addition, as organisations grow and expand, it may be necessary to review key governance areas including the organisation's mandate, composition and structure of governing bodies, and relationships with key stakeholders.

The importance of governance frameworks is widely recognised by various governance institutions and stakeholders. For example, the Australian Institute of Company Directors states:

> The governance attributes of an organisation are shaped by a variety of factors, both 'internal' (e.g. constitution, organisational policies) and 'external' (e.g. laws, regulations, community expectations) ... A common goal for organisations is to have the most effective governance framework in place that best meets their individual circumstances and needs – helping to drive enhanced organisational performance while at the same time aiding conformance with various requirements (e.g. the company's constitution, policies, controls and procedures as well as with applicable external regulations and laws).

Internal governance frameworks

There are different types of organisations and therefore the frameworks for internal governance vary depending on the nature of the organisation. These include companies, trusts, partnerships, statutory bodies/agencies, not-for-profit organisations and charities. In companies and other organisations that are established as legal entities, the first point of call is the constitution/charter/Articles.

The Articles/charter/constitution of an organisation

All organisations that are formally established through a process of incorporation or registration have Articles/charter/constitution that prescribe the internal governance arrangements of the organisation. Section 17 of the 2006 Companies Act of the United Kingdom defines a company's constitution to mean its Articles. Section 18 further states that a company must have Articles of Association prescribing regulations for the company, and a company is required to register its Articles (where the articles are not registered, section 20 provides for default application of the model articles).

As stated in section 18(1) of the Companies Act, the primary purpose of the Articles is to prescribe regulations for the company. Section 33 of the Act further states that the provisions of a company's constitution bind the company and its members to the same extent as if there were covenants on the part of the company and of each member to observe those provisions. Some leading corporate law scholars such as Eilis Ferran state that in the UK, it is the Articles of Association that now constitute the main constitutional document (of a company), although there may be other relevant documents such as shareholder agreements.

Matters provided for in the Articles/constitution/charter of a company include the governance structure and levels of authority or division of power among the governance bodies such as the shareholders, board of directors and management. Various corporate governance standards require clarity of roles between the various organs within an organisation, most often between the board and management. The primary instrument where the clarity should be provided is the Articles/constitution/charter. Other matters contained in the Articles/constitution/charter include participation rights (such as voting and non-voting shares/stock), reporting frameworks and accountability measures.

After incorporation or registration of an organisation, the foundation documents such as the Articles/constitution/charter are often shelved and yet these play an important governance role because they provide the primary framework for internal governance. Key provisions that are important for organisational governance are:

- purpose of the organisation;
- nature and structure of the organisation;
- governing bodies and their roles and responsibilities; and
- ownership rights and participation rights.

Several organisations recognise that the Articles/constitution/charter provide the primary governance framework. For example, PepsiCo identifies its Articles as the source of the structure and purpose of the organisation, and by-laws as proving the rights and powers of shareholders, directors and officers.

> Corporate Governance
>
> Amended and Restated Articles of Incorporation
>
> PepsiCo's articles of incorporation provide a legal declaration of our structure and purpose as corporation as mandate by North Carolina law.
>
> By-Laws
>
> PepsiCo's By-Laws spell out the rules and procedures by which we operate as well as the rights and powers of company shareholders, directors and officers.

The Companies (Model Articles) Regulations of 2008 were made pursuant to section 19 of the UK Companies Act of 2006; they provide model articles for private companies limited by shares, companies limited by guarantee and public companies. Although companies are not obliged to adopt model articles, these provide the general framework for the Articles of a company and contain various provisions on key internal governance matters such as the role and structure of the board, decision making and conflicts of interest.

The role of the board

Article 3 provides that subject to the Articles, the directors are responsible for the management of the company's business, for which purpose they may exercise all the powers of the company. This article provides the basis for the mandate and general scope of powers of directors. Corporate governance standards on the role of the board build on this to clarify the roles and responsibilities of the board. For example, the principle on leadership in the UK Corporate Governance Code provides that every company should be headed by an effective board which is collectively responsible for the long-term success of the company.

Structure of the board

Article 5 permits directors to delegate any of the powers conferred on them under the Articles to a person or committee in such manner and terms as they think fit. Article 6 further provides that committees to which directors delegate their powers must follow procedures which are based, as far as applicable, on those provisions of the Articles that govern taking decisions by directors. Committees enable boards to function effectively.

Decision making

Article 7 provides the general rule on decision making by directors – that is, a majority or unanimous decision. Several principles flow from this, including collective decision making, transparency and ensuring that boards are not dominated by a single person.

Conflicts of interest

Article 16 provides procedures for managing conflicts of interest of directors in relation to transactions in which they have an interest. These include the requirement to disclose interests, the role of the board in determining the nature of interest and non-participation by the conflicted director in decisions on transactions in which he or she has an interest. Corporate governance standards have built on this to provide principles and standards on ethical leadership and transparency in decision making.

The Articles/charter/constitution of an organisation are one of the internal governance mechanisms and their role, as indicated above, is to provide the general framework for governance of the organisation.

Shareholder agreements

A shareholder agreement is an agreement between some or all of the shareholders of a company. It is a control-enhancing mechanism, contractual in nature and only binding on the parties to it. Shareholder agreements seek to create binding obligations on matters that are likely to cause conflict, such as governance arrangements including structure and composition of the board, pre-emption rights, dilution and exit. These agreements have historically been used in financing arrangements such as venture capital where equity financiers use shareholder agreements to manage relationships with owner-managers.

The status of shareholder agreements in relation to other internal governance frameworks such as the Articles of Association has been clarified by the courts in the UK. In *Patrick Giles Gauntlet Dear and Read Eugine Griffith v Alexander Edward Jackson [2013] EWCA Civ 89*, the appellants who held a combined controlling stake (60%) in Polygon Credit Holdings II Limited (PCH II), the sole voting shareholder of Tetragon Financial Group Limited (TFG) had entered into an agreement not to invoke certain provisions of the Articles of Association of TFG or any other power to remove Mr Jackson as director, provided termination event had not occurred. In 2011, Mr Jackson was removed as director and challenged the removal on grounds of breach of the agreement. The essence of his argument was that the two shareholders, who were also directors, were bound by the agreement in the exercise of their powers as directors. The respondents relied on the powers to remove a director in the Articles of Association of the company. The Court of Appeal, reversing a decision of the High Court, held that shareholders are bound by any agreements entered into and are at liberty to act in their interests. However, a shareholder's agreement cannot limit the powers of directors as provided for in the Articles of Association, since directors act in the best interests of the company. The implications of this decision are that while shareholders' agreements are valid and a matter of freedom of contract, they do not override a company's Articles.

Research has shown that although permitted by legal frameworks in several jurisdictions, the use of shareholder agreements varies across jurisdictions. They are common in the United States and Canada and in some European countries, particularly Italy, France and Belgium.

Shareholder agreements revolve around shareholder relations and this is a key corporate governance matter thus making shareholder agreements part of the internal governance frameworks of an organisation. The range of issues covered in the agreements is wide but key issues relate to:

- the business of the organisation;
- governance arrangements such as structure and composition of the board;
- control and management of the organisation;
- decision making and dispute resolution;
- access to information;

- financing, pre-emption rights, sharing of profits and exit arrangements;
- intellectual property rights;
- minority rights and dilution; and
- competition

Shareholder agreements may enhance or undermine corporate governance. To the extent that they are used as a control-enhancing mechanism, they distort shareholder relations and increase potential for negative activities associated with control such as expropriation. On the other hand, they are considered a key corporate governance tool, particularly in relation to internal governance arrangements, shareholder relations and dispute resolution.

Governance arrangements

Shareholder agreements prescribe internal governance arrangements, particularly the structure and composition of the board and the role of various stakeholders in board appointments. In organisations that have controlling shareholders, shareholder representation on the board and appointment of directors may cause conflict and to the extent that such matters are clearly articulated in shareholder agreements, provides clarity and prevents future conflict.

Shareholder relations and minority protection

Corporate governance standards recognise the implications of ownership and governance, particularly in relation to controlling and minority shareholders. The G20/OCED Principles of Corporate Governance provide for equitable treatment of shareholders. Therefore, shareholder agreements may provide mechanisms for minority shareholder protection such as voting pacts and veto rights and generally provide the framework for shareholder relations, enhancing governance within an organisation. Some scholars such as Versiliki Stergiou have argued that shareholder agreements constitute a central factor in the relationship of multiple large shareholder ownership structures and corporate governance.

Dispute resolution

The main purpose of shareholder agreements is to prevent disputes. The agreements often provide for mechanisms for resolving matters where there is disagreement or when actual disputes arise. The mechanisms vary and include a casting vote by an independent chairman, referring matters to an independent party, and arbitration in relation to specific or all disputes.

Shareholder agreements seek to regulate other issues, such as transfer of shares, pre-emption rights, dilution, tag-along and drag-along rights. This is all within the content of shareholder relations. The extent to which they enhance or undermine governance depends on broader governance frameworks, particularly external frameworks such as legal and regulatory frameworks that govern organisations and specifically investor protection.

Organisational policies and codes

These guide the day-to-day operations of an organisation and include the following.

Codes of ethics

Corporate governance standards place the responsibility for ethics on the governing bodies which are required to ensure that an organisation has a code of ethics, among other things. A code of ethics provides the framework for ethical conduct for both the governing body and management. It also communicates to shareholders and other stakeholders and organisations values and standards of conduct in all transactions. Chapter 6 provides a detailed discussion of ethics.

Financial management policies

Financial management policies contain some of the key internal controls within an organisation and are particularly important for safeguarding an organisation's resources. They provide for matters such as procedures for payments, cash management, records of financial transactions and reporting requirements such as quarterly, semi-annual and annual reports. Financial and other reports aid decision making at various levels within an organisation and therefore financial management policies play an important governance role.

The relationship between financial management and corporate governance is circular. Good financial management aids decision making and improves governance. In turn, corporate governance leads to improved financial management.

Human resource policies

For all organisations, people are the most important resource. Employees are key stakeholders and therefore human resource management is a key aspect of governance. Key areas include transparent processes for recruitment, remuneration, learning and development, induction and orientation, and compliance with labour laws and standards, as well as policies dealing with issues such as discrimination and harassment. The policies help organisations to manage their most important resource – people – and to protect the image of the organisation.

Other internal policies include procurement and supply chain management policies, whistleblower policies and client charters.

Key points to remember about policies are that they should:

- reflect the values of the organisation;
- inform and guide operations;
- be communicated internally and externally through induction and regular training of staff, on company websites and contract documents;
- be living documents – that is, operations should be aligned with policies and they should be periodically reviewed to ensure they are up to date; and
- be complied with through clear mechanisms put in place by the organisation.

For non-listed and non-regulated organisations, internal governance frameworks are largely determined by the organisation.

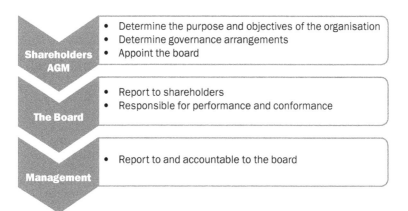

Figure 2.2: Key governing bodies and their roles

It is important for organisations to ensure that internal governance frameworks are effective. This includes ensuring key governance documents align governance structures with best practice standards such as providing for clarity of roles between the different governing bodies and representation of key stakeholders on governing bodies. Figure 2.2 illustrates the internal governance structure of an organisation and the roles of the key governing bodies.

Figure 2.3 outlines measures to ensure effectiveness of internal governance.

Shareholders/ AGM

- Clarity of roles in the articles/constitution/charter
- Diversity of ownership
- Governance practices of institutional shareholders (*e.g. disclosure of ownership and voting practices, measures to manage conflicts of interest and regulate related party transactions*)
- Effective monitoring mechanisms (*external audit function, financial reporting and disclosure standards*)
- Strong legal frameworks and effective redress mechanisms
- Measures to enhance shareholder democracy (*proxy rights, participation in absentia, shareholder forums*)
- Strong information and reporting frameworks

Board of directors

- Transparent appointment processes
- Ethical leadership
- Structure and composition (*that allows for diversity of skill and representation of key stakeholders*)
- Overall functioning (*committees, information, performance evaluation*)

Management

- Control environment and processes (*operations, reporting and compliance*)

Figure 2.3: Measures to ensure the effectiveness of internal governance bodies

External governance frameworks

External governance frameworks include laws, regulations and standards that organisations are required to comply with, and these vary depending on the nature of the organisation. Legal and regulatory frameworks provide the overarching architecture for corporate governance. This is best illustrated by Principle 1 of the G20/OECD Principles of Corporate Governance, ensuring the basis for an effective corporate governance framework. According to the OECD, key aspects of an effective framework are promoting transparent and fair markets, efficient allocation of resources, consistency with rule of law and supporting effective supervision and enforcement.

Legal and regulatory frameworks

These include laws that govern the formation and incorporation of organisations such as company law, trust law, partnership law and other laws which shall collectively be referred to as organisational law. Other legal and regulatory frameworks include securities laws and corporate governance standards for regulated entities such as banks, insurance and pension funds.

Organisational laws

We use the term organisational laws in a broad sense to mean laws that provide for the establishment or incorporation of organisations. These include companies, partnerships, cooperatives and not-for-profit organisations, among others. The laws simply prescribe not just procedures for establishing the organisations but also allocation of authority and participation rights. Organisational laws provide the framework for establishing governance structures and allocating roles and responsibilities between shareholders, the board and management.

The fundamental role of organisational laws is that they provide the primary governance framework for organisations. Company law, for example, provides procedures for establishing companies, the internal governance institutions/organs (shareholders, directors and management), the framework for managing relations between and among the governance institutions including assigning roles and responsibilities, accountability and redress mechanisms.

The quality of organisational laws and quality of enforcement are critical for governance. As the primary governance frameworks, it is important that the laws provide clear and adequate standards on ownership and participation rights, leadership, information and accountability. In all jurisdictions, legal frameworks such as company law provide the primary governance framework for organisations, particularly those that are not listed on stock markets, which are always the majority. Therefore, it is important to ensure that the law adequately covers key governance matters such as internal governance structures, fiduciary duties, information rights, and existing mechanisms and measures for seeking redress in case of wrongs against the participants (such as oppression and prejudicial conduct) as well as against the entity (such as derivative actions).

Commenting on the governance role of company law, governance scholars such as Erik P.M. Vermulen argue that company law is the most important source of corporate governance in the context of non-listed companies, which are the majority in most economies, and thus plays an important role of providing mechanisms to impede opportunistic behaviour.

Securities laws

Securities markets enable corporations and other organisations to raise capital publicly. This creates a situation where providers of capital are not involved in the day-to-day activities or management of the organisation. The objective of securities regulation is to protect providers of capital (otherwise known as investors) as well as ensure fair and stable markets by prescribing regulatory standards for those who seek to raise capital (issuers of securities), professionals and other participants in securities markets (such as transaction advisors, brokers and asset managers).

The International Organisation of Securities Commission (IOSCO) issued a statement of objectives and principles of securities markets regulation that outlines three overarching objectives:
- protecting investors;
- ensuring that markets are fair, efficient and transparent; and
- reducing systemic risk.

The legal and regulatory frameworks of securities markets seek to achieve the above objectives through various measures including:
- prescribing disclosure standards that are in line with corporate governance principles on transparency;

- enforcing financial reporting standards that ensure fair, timely and accurate disclosure of information; and
- prohibiting insider dealing and other market abuse practices.

These measures enhance transparency and governance of issuers of securities and other securities markets participants.

The G20/OECD Principles recognise the need for stock markets to function in a manner that contributes to good governance and in particular in relation to frameworks that prescribe governance standards for institutional investors and measures to minimise conflict of interest by securities markets participants. These include:

- governance and voting arrangements of institutional investors;
- disclosure of measures to manage conflicts of interest by institutional investors acting in a fiduciary capacity;
- disclosure and management of conflicts of interests by market participants;
- prohibition and enforcement of insider trading and market manipulation rules;
- disclosure of corporate governance standards of the primary jurisdiction of listed entities; and
- the role of stock markets in providing fair and efficient price discovery as a means to promote effective corporate governance.

Accounting and financial reporting frameworks

Accountability and transparency are key corporate governance principles. All organisations need robust frameworks for financial management and reporting. Organisations are entrusted with resources from various stakeholders such as owners/founders, creditors, clients and investors. Financial management practices enable organisations to safeguard and utilise those resources for proper purpose. On the other hand, financial reporting standards ensure that organisations provide timely and accurate information.

Some primary governance frameworks such as company laws provide the framework and responsibility for accounting and financial reporting. Part 15 of the UK Companies Act of 2006 has provisions on accounts and reports that include duty to keep accounting records in section 386, a company's financial year in section 389, the requirement for accounts to give a true and fair view in section 393, publication of accounts and records in section 423, laying of accounts and reports before general meeting in section 437, and filing of accounts and reports in section 442.

Both the Companies Act and corporate governance standards place the responsibility for financial reporting on the governing body – the board of directors (see section 393). In addition, section 394 states clearly the responsibilities of directors.

393 Accounts to give true and fair view

(1) The directors of a company must not approve accounts for the purposes of this chapter unless they are satisfied that they give a true and fair view of the assets, liabilities, financial position and profit or loss—

    (a) in the case of the company's individual accounts, of the company;

    (b) in the case of the company's group accounts, of the undertakings included in the consolidation as a whole, so far as concerns members of the company.

(2) The auditor of a company in carrying out his functions under this Act in relation to the company's annual accounts must have regard to the directors' duty under subsection (1).

394 Duty to prepare individual accounts

The directors of every company must prepare accounts for the company for each of its financial years.

Those accounts are referred to as the company's 'individual accounts'.

The UK Corporate Governance Code 2018 places the responsibility for financial reporting on the board as well as broadening the scope to include reporting on the company's prospects. The principle states:

> The board should present a fair, balanced and understandable assessment of the company's position and prospects, and satisfy itself on the integrity of financial information.

The Code further provides guidance on the scope of director's responsibilities in relation to financial and business reporting. These include the requirement to provide an explanation of the basis on which the company generates or preserves value over the longer term (the business model) and the strategy for delivering the objectives of the company. In addition, the directors should state whether they consider it appropriate to adopt the going concern basis of accounting in preparing them, and identify any material uncertainties to the company's ability to continue to do so over a period of at least 12 months from the date of approval of the financial statements.

Corporate governance codes

Codes of corporate governance gained prominence in the 1990s following a series of governance failures or corporate scandals in various jurisdictions. Some of the early codes developed in response to governance failures were the 1992 Financial Aspects of Corporate Governance (Cadbury Committee Report), the 1994 King 1 Report on Corporate Governance (South Africa), the 1999 Commonwealth Association for Corporate Governance (CACG) Guidelines: Principles for Corporate Governance in the Commonwealth and the 2004 OECD Principles of Corporate Governance.

The emergence of corporate governance codes was an important milestone in the development of corporate governance for the following reasons:

- they raised the bar for corporate governance by generating debate and discussion on the subject and it was evident from the codes that there was a high level of convergence in relation to the fundamental principles of corporate governance.
- The codes served as key reference points for organisations and boards.
- The codes, particularly the OCED Principles, provide a benchmark for assessing corporate governance standards. As stated in the note to the principles by the OECD Secretary General, 'The principles have a proven record as the international reference point and as an effective tool for implementation.' The Secretary General cites adoption of the Principles by the Financial Stability Board (FSB) as part of the standards for sound financial systems for FSB, G20 and OECD members. In addition, he states that the Principles have been used by the World Bank Group in more than 60 country reviews worldwide, and that they also serve as the basis for the guidelines on corporate governance of banks issued by the Basel Committee on banking supervision, the OECD Guidelines on insurer and pension fund governance, and as a reference for reform in individual countries.
- They influenced the development of corporate governance standards in various sectors and jurisdictions such as principles for

multinationals, not-for-profit organisations, education institutions and the health sector among others.

- The codes articulated the roles and responsibilities of the board and continue to provide guidance on director appointments, board structure and composition, board effectiveness.
- They provided clarity on the roles of the board and management.
- They provided a catalyst for research and studies on governance practices and behaviour.
- They provide the basis for establishing the link between governance and sustainability.

Corporate governance codes are part of the external governance framework for organisations. They provide best practice standards on key governance issues such as: appointment, composition, roles and responsibilities of governing bodies; risk management and internal controls; stakeholder relations; reporting and accountability. A key feature of codes is that they are subject to periodic revisions, taking into account emerging issues and thus providing guidance to organisations and governing bodies to align their governance practices with emerging best practice standards.

In the UK, in July 2018, the Financial Reporting Council of the UK released the 2018 Corporate Governance code after extensive consultations and focuses on the key elements of long term sustainable growth for organisations and the economy. These are leadership, culture, and stakeholder relations.

In South Africa, the most recent code, KING IV, cites various factors that influenced the development of the code including:

a) new global realities testing the leadership of organisations on issues as diverse as inequality, globalised trade, social tensions, climate change, population growth, ecological overshoot, geopolitical tensions, radical transparency and rapid technological and scientific advancement;

b) global factors such as financial instability, climate change, pressures on natural resources, social media, and technology disruptions; and

c) the three shifts in the corporate world – from financial capitalism to unclassified capitalism; from short-term capital markets to long-term sustainable capital markets; and from siloed reporting to integrated reporting.

External governance frameworks are not determined by an individual organisation but are part of the overall governance architecture. Their effectiveness depends on factors outside the organisation and includes national policy and enforcement capacity. Governments have a role to play in ensuring the adequacy and effectiveness of external governance frameworks, including periodically reviewing them to ensure they are responsive to the needs of the market and ensuring the relevant institutions have the resources to enforce them. Individual organisations are required to comply and align internal governance with regulatory and other external governance requirements.

Chapter summary

- The governance framework for organisations comprises both internal and external frameworks.
- The effectiveness of both internal and external governance frameworks is key for corporate governance. Weaknesses in one cannot be compensated for by fully adopting or embracing the other.
- Some studies have shown positive benefits for firms in jurisdictions with legal and enforcement frameworks that adopt good internal governance practices. However, internal governance cannot fully compensate for the absence of robust external governance frameworks.

3   Evolution of corporate governance

Introduction

This chapter describes the evolution of corporate governance from its origins in the UK, how it has developed as a discipline, internationally across the globe, sector by sector and also by organisational type.

Origins of corporate governance

Corporate governance has developed piecemeal around the globe, often in reaction to corporate scandals. As it develops it creates new laws, regulations and codes at national, regional, sector-specific and international levels. We saw in Chapter 1 that corporate governance originally developed in the early 1990s as a principles-based voluntary approach which was self-regulated by the owners of organisations. Since then, more and more countries have adopted rules-based regulations to compensate for the lack of or failure of self-regulation.

Corporate governance, in the developed world, is still viewed as a protector of shareholder value and of investors, whereas in developing countries, it is seen as a mechanism for creating economic growth and poverty eradication through the creation of better-run and thus better-performing sustainable organisations.

Corporate governance is also spreading its application from listed companies to organisations in all sectors – private, public and not-for-profit – so that schools, hospitals, sporting bodies and faith-based organisations are now all talking about corporate governance. It is raising the question whether 'corporate governance' is still the correct term for this phenomenon or whether the 21st century will see it being re-christened with a new name. Suggestions include 'governance of organisations' or 'enterprise governance', to reflect the fact that governance practices are being adopted by more than just corporates.

Corporate governance scandals are not new. The first recorded incidents of corporate governance malpractices occurred in the eighteenth century with the British East India Company and the South Sea Company.

The British East India Company had been established in 1600 by royal charter to help merchants and explorers establish trade on behalf of England in the East. The charter granted limited liability to the East India Company investors. The company rose to global domination in both business and government as it extended its operations from trade to obtain territory. Over the years, the East India Company controlled and ruled territories either directly or indirectly via local puppet rulers, owned private armies exercising power and administrative functions, and monopolised exports of products such as opium and tea. By 1784, the East India Company had become so corrupt that the British government nationalised it through the India Act of 1784.

In 1720, speculators in the stock of the South Sea Company created the South Sea Bubble, an economic bubble where the price of the stock was considerably higher than the intrinsic value of the company. When the bubble burst, it left many in financial ruin.

However, as we saw in Chapter 1, it was a number of company collapses in the UK – most notably Polly Peck International (1990), the Bank of Credit and Commerce International (1991), the Mirror Group News International (1991) and Barings Bank (1995) – in the late 1980s and early 1990s that created an impetus for better practices in Corporate Governance in the UK. In each case, there seemed to be serious accounting or financial reporting irregularities and inadequate internal controls and risk management. When questions were asked about how corporate collapses could happen to such well-established companies without warning, some common themes emerged:

- Investors were not kept informed about what was really going on in the company.
- The published financial statements were misleading.
- External auditors were accused of failing to spot the warning signs.
- The companies had self-seeking powerful chiefs, who lacked business ethics.
- Board members were unable to restrain management from acting improperly.
- Risk management systems were inadequate or ineffective.

The London Stock Exchange asked Sir Adrian Cadbury to set up a committee representing major financial market institutions to look into the financial aspects of corporate governance, amid concerns that financial reporting by companies was often misleading. The Committee broadened its scope to include other aspects of corporate governance, particularly the functions and effectiveness of the board of directors. The 'Report of the Committee on the Financial Aspects of Corporate Governance: The Code of Best Practice' (the Cadbury Report) was published in 1992. The London Stock Exchange introduced a requirement into its Listing Rules that listed companies should include a statement of compliance with the Code of Best Practice in their Annual Report and Accounts. The statement of compliance required an explanation of where the company had complied with the code of best practice and in circumstances where it had not an explanation as to why not.

One could argue that the provisions relating to the topics covered in the Cadbury Report (set out on page 43) have become the foundation stones for international best practice in corporate governance as known today. Each has been developed further as best practice, and thinking on the subject has evolved to where we are today. In addition, new provisions such as those for shareholders and stakeholder engagement have been added.

Topics covered by the Cadbury Report include:
- board effectiveness;
- the chairman;
- non-executive directors;
- professional advice;
- directors' training;
- board structures and procedures;
- the company secretary;
- directors' responsibilities;
- standards of conduct;
- nominations committees;
- audit committees;
- internal financial controls;
- internal audit; and
- board remuneration.

UK corporate governance

The Cadbury Report

Board of directors

The Committee agreed that the balance of power between directors and shareholders was appropriate, but that there should be more accountability by directors to shareholders. Control over the company should be exercised collectively by the board as a whole. There should be no domination by a single individual. There should be a separate chairman and chief executive, and both should have clearly defined roles. The board should have reserved matters which should not be delegated to management. The board should meet regularly and should monitor the performance of the executive management. Individual board members should be able to seek professional advice at the company's expense. This recognised the risk that some directors might not have the necessary experience or skills in a particular area to play an effective role in a particular discussion.

Non-executive directors

At the time of the Cadbury Report, non-executive directors were not common. Those that did exist were major shareholder appointments or former executives. The Committee recommended that there should be sufficient non-executive directors for their views to carry weight, and most of them should be independent. Independent non-executive directors should be able to bring judgement and experience to the deliberations of the board that the executive directors on their own might lack. Non-executive directors should be selected through a formal process overseen by a nominations committee. Recommendations would then be made to the board, who would formally appoint them. Their appointment would be for a fixed term, and their reappointment should not be automatic. Although the Cadbury Report Committee did not set maximum terms for non-executive directors, it did imply that they became less independent over time.

Executive directors

The Committee recommended that directors' service contracts should not exceed three years without shareholder approval. This was to reduce large payouts for poor performance. At this time, there was not the debate about directors' remuneration and pay for failure that we see in many countries today. The Committee also recommended that directors' remuneration should be decided by a remuneration committee consisting wholly or mainly of non-executives.

The audit committee

The Committee recommended that all listed companies should have an audit committee, and set out its remit. The audit committee should comprise at least three non-executives and should be the main relationship with the external auditors. Previously the external auditors' main relationship had been with executive management. The audit committee should also review the interim and annual financial statements before their submission to the full board for approval.

A 'going concern' statement

The Committee recommended that companies should include a 'going concern' statement in their annual report and accounts. An implication of this recommendation is that before approving the report and accounts, each director is under a personal responsibility to reassure himself or herself that the company is a going concern and is not on the brink of insolvency.

Internal financial controls

Directors should also report to shareholders on the internal financial controls.

The Cadbury Report therefore introduced for FTSE 350 companies the requirements for non-executive directors, independent directors, audit, nomination and remuneration committees, evaluation of performance and reports on the internal controls of a company.

Directors' Remuneration: Report of a Study Group chaired by Sir Richard Greenbury (Greenbury Report)

In 1995, due to directors' remuneration becoming a problematic issue in the UK, a committee was set up under the chairmanship of Sir Richard Greenbury to look into the issue. The following is a summary of the Greenbury Report's recommendations:

- The remuneration committee of the board should decide the remuneration of the executive directors.
- The Committee should comprise entirely non-executive directors, so that no executive director has responsibility for setting his or her own or the remuneration of executive colleagues.
- Maximum notice periods in executive directors' contracts should normally be 12 months. However, two-year notice periods may be acceptable in exceptional circumstances to entice a key individual to join a board.
- Executive pay should not be excessive but remuneration packages should be sufficient to attract, retain and motivate individuals of the required quality. One could argue that this gave remuneration committees carte blanche when setting packages because any package can be justified on the grounds that it was needed in order to attract a person of the necessary calibre.
- The concept of performance-related pay being closely linked with the interests of shareholders was introduced. The performance criteria should be relevant, stretching and designed to enhance the business.
- Matters for the remuneration committee to consider should include the phasing of any reward schemes, the nature of any share option packages and the implications of each element of the remuneration package for payments into the directors' pension plans.
- Share option awards should be phased into smaller payments and should not be issued at a discount.
- Remuneration committees were tasked with taking a firmer line on payments to directors dismissed for unsatisfactory performance. In practice this was difficult, as outgoing directors could still insist that a company honour its contractual obligations set out in the service contract.
- Listed companies were required to disclose information about their remuneration policy and the remuneration of their individual directors in a remuneration report in the company's annual report and accounts.
- The chairman of the remuneration committee should attend the annual general meeting of shareholders each year in order to provide some accountability to shareholders.

Hampel Report and Combined Code

In 1996, the Hampel Committee was set up to review corporate governance practices in the UK following the introduction of the Codes from the Cadbury and Greenbury Reports. The result in 1998 was the publication of the Hampel Report, which led to the introduction of the Combined Code of Corporate Governance in the UK.

Hampel proposed the introduction of a code based on principles, which would hopefully restrict the regulatory burden on companies. Companies were required to 'comply or explain' why they did not comply with the principles set out in the code. This approach, which recognises the need for flexibility due to the diversity of circumstances and experiences within companies and the fact that non-compliance may at that time in a company's life cycle be in its best interests, still endures today in the UK and has been adopted in many other countries.

The Combined Code also included, for the first time, principles and a code of practice for institutional shareholders. The aim was to encourage institutional shareholders to take a more active role in the governance of those companies in which they invest. It was argued that institutional shareholders, such as pension funds, unit trusts and life assurance companies, hold funds on behalf of many individuals and are therefore investing indirectly on behalf of those individuals. They thus have a responsibility on behalf of those individuals to make sure that the board of directors of the companies in which these individuals invest are made properly accountable and govern their companies responsibly.

Institutional shareholders should have a dialogue with the companies in which they invest and make their views known, through advisory reports and, if necessary, via their voting practices at shareholder meetings.

The UK Combined Code was updated in 2003 by the Higgs and Smith Reports and in 2006 by the Financial Reporting Council (FRC). The aim has been to strengthen the provisions and disclosures surrounding non-executive directors, to make institutional shareholders more accountable and to give guidance on the role of Audit Committees and the responsibilities of their members.

The disclosure requirements for directors' remuneration set out in the Combined Code led in 2002 to the amendment of the Companies Act by the Directors' Remuneration Report Regulations. These Regulations were amended in 2013. The requirements introduced in 2013 are discussed later in this chapter.

Internal Control: Guidance for Directors on the Combined Code (Turnbull Report)

The UK Corporate Governance Code states that 'the board should maintain sound risk management and internal control systems' and that 'the Board should, at least annually, conduct a review of the effectiveness of the company's risk management and internal control systems and should report to shareholders that they have done so. The review should cover all material controls, including financial, operational, and compliance controls.' The Turnbull Report, issued in 1999, gave directors guidance on carrying out this review. In 2005, revised guidance on the Turnbull Report was published. There were few substantive changes but boards were encouraged to review their application of the guidance on a continuing basis and to look on the internal control statement as an opportunity to communicate to their shareholders how they manage risk and internal control. They should notify shareholders, in the annual report, of how any significant failings or weaknesses in the effectiveness of the internal control system have been dealt with.

The Turnbull Report has now been replaced by the FRC's 'Guidance on Risk Management, Internal Control and Related Financial Business Reporting' (Guidance) which was published in 2014. The aim of this Guidance was to bring together all of the previous guidance for best practice in risk management: the Financial Reporting Council's (FRC) 'Internal Control: Revised Guidance for Directors on the Combined Code' and 'Going Concern and Liquidity Risk: Guidance for Directors of UK Companies', and reflects changes made to the UK Corporate Governance Code. It also links the Turnbull guidance on internal control with emerging good practice for risk management reflected in the conclusions of both the FRC's Boards and Risk report, issued in September 2011, and the final recommendations of the Sharman Panel of Inquiry into Going Concern and Liquidity Risk, issued in March 2011.

The Guidance:
- prompts boards to consider how to discharge their responsibilities in relation to the existing and emerging principal risks faced by the company;

- encourages organisations to reflect sound business practice, whereby risk management and internal control are embedded in the business process by which a company pursues its objectives;
- encourages the creation of the appropriate risk cultures within organisation based on the board's agreed risk appetite and tolerance for the organisation. This means going further than the traditional mechanical risk management process; and
- highlights related reporting responsibilities.

Institutional Investment in the UK: A Review (HM Treasury 2001, updated 2007) (Myners Reports)

Lord Myners chaired working groups which looked into the relationship between companies and institutional investors in 1995, 2001, 2004 and 2007. The recommendations from these working groups were incorporated into the UK Combined Code. They included suggestions for improving communications between companies and their shareholders, and urged institutional shareholders to reassess their role as shareholders, especially their role in respective of good governance. Companies were also encouraged to carry out their voting by way of a poll, so that the votes of all institutional shareholders were counted whether they attended a general meeting or not.

Review on the Role and Effectiveness of Non-Executive Directors (The UK Department of Trade and Industry 2003) (Higgs Report)

The UK Department of Trade and Industry asked Sir Derek Higgs to set up a Committee to review the role and effectiveness of non-executive directors. The Higgs Report was first published in January 2003 and reviewed in 2006 by ICSA ('Improving Board Effectiveness'). In July 2018, the Financial Reporting Council (FRC) issued Guidance on Board Effectiveness, the primary purpose of which 'is to stimulate boards' thinking on how they can carry out their role and encourage them to focus on continually improving their effectiveness'.

The Higgs Report looked at the role and effectiveness of non-executive directors. Many of the report's recommendations were incorporated into the Combined Code or appended to the Code in the 'Suggestions for Good Practices'.

The Higgs Report concluded that the role of a non-executive director had four elements:

1. Strategy: non-executive directors should constructively challenge and help to develop proposals on strategy.
2. Performance: non-executive directors should scrutinise the performance of executive management in achieving agreed goals and objectives, and monitor the reporting of performance.
3. Risk: non-executive directors should satisfy themselves about the integrity of financial information and that the systems of internal control and risk management are robust.
4. People: non-executive directors are responsible for deciding the level of remuneration for executive directors and should have a prime role in succession planning for the board.

The Higgs Report also introduced the concept of a senior independent director and a definition for directors' 'independence'.

The good practices suggested by Higgs have also been adopted by many other countries as the basis for their corporate governance codes and best practices.

Audit Committees: Combined Code Guidance (Smith Report)

Also in January 2003, the Financial Reporting Council published the Smith Report to give guidance to boards on how to organise their audit committees, and to members of audit committees on their roles and responsibilities. The Guidance was appended to the Combined Code.

The FRC Guidance for Audit Committees was updated in April 2016. It is intended to assist company boards when implementing Section C.3 of the UK Corporate Governance Code 2016, which deals with audit committees and auditors, and to assist directors serving on audit committees in carrying out their role.

The FRC has also provided a Best Practice Guide to Audit Tendering (2016), to assist audit committees looking to put their external audit out to tender.

Report on the Recruitment and Development of Non-Executive Directors 2006 (Tyson Report)

Following publication of the Higgs Report, the Department of Trade and Industry set up a task force under the Chair of Laura Tyson, the Dean of the London Business School, to look into the recruitment and development of non-executive directors. The Tyson Report was published in June 2006 and argued that a range of different experiences and backgrounds among board members can enhance the effectiveness of the board. It suggests how a broader range of non-executive directors can be identified and recruited.

Sources of non-executive directors highlighted in the report included:

1. the 'marzipan layer' of corporate management, just below the board level;
2. individuals in private sector companies;
3. individuals in the public sector/non-commercial sector; and
4. individuals working for business consultancies or professional firms (lawyers and accountants) and retired professional accountants.

Further research and initiatives on diversity of board members are discussed below.

The Companies Act 2006

Statutory duties for directors

The Companies Act 2006 (the Act) introduced statutory duties for directors. These duties were similar to the previous duties which had existed under common law and equity in the UK. A list of the statutory duties of directors can be seen in the box below. The Act also introduced a requirement for companies to issue an annual strategic review in narrative form. It was hoped that this would make companies more accountable to their shareholders.

THE STATUTORY DUTIES OF DIRECTORS UNDER THE COMPANIES ACT 2016

- To act within powers.
- To promote the success of the company.
- To exercise independent judgement.
- To exercise reasonable care, skill and diligence.
- To avoid conflict of interests.
- To not accept benefits from third parties.
- To declare any interest in a proposed transaction or arrangement.

Shareholder communications

The Companies Act 2006 introduced the following provisions into law relating to how a company communicates with its shareholders.

- Documents and information are now able to be sent by or to companies either in hard copy form or electronic form, i.e. email or fax. Under the Transparency Rules, listed companies need to obtain a shareholder resolution for communications to be sent by email and fax.
- Companies are also permitted, if a shareholder has not opted-out, to communicate with their shareholders by means of a website. Notifications of any such communications will have to be sent in hard copy unless the shareholder has assented to receiving them by email or fax. The use of the company's website for shareholder communications requires the passing of a shareholders' resolution or permission in the company's articles.
- Shareholders always have the right to ask for a hard copy of the communications they receive electronically.

Enfranchising indirect shareholders

The Companies Act 2006 aims to assist indirect investors – i.e. share-owners who hold shares through one or more financial intermediary – to become more involved in the company's affairs through access to information, and the exercise of rights normally reserved for registered share-holders. The Act seeks to achieve this through:

- enabling registered shareholders to nominate another person to exercise or enjoy all or any of the shareholder rights, including voting rights, so long as a provision to that effect is included in the company's articles. Few companies have changed their articles so the impact of this provision is not material; and
- giving beneficial shareholders direct rights to company information. The right is not automatic and requires the registered shareholder to nominate the indirect investor. Where this has happened, many listed companies do provide notifications of when information has been made available on the company's website direct to the indirect investor. Where a notice of a meeting is sent to an indirect investor, the company will usually alert the indirect investor to the fact that they may have the right to be appointed a proxy for the meeting.

Voting

The Companies Act 2006 extended the statutory rights to proxies. Shareholders are now able to appoint more than one proxy per share-holding, as long as each proxy represents a different part of the appointor's holding. Proxies are able to exercise all or any of the rights of shareholders to attend, speak and vote at a meeting on a show of hands or on a poll for the part of the holding they represent.

The UK Corporate Governance Code

Following the financial crisis in the UK which came to a head in 2008–09, Sir David Walker was asked to review governance in banks and other financial institutions. His findings led to the Financial Reporting Council (FRC) instigating a review of the Combined Code. The FRC review concluded that more attention needed to be paid by boards 'to follow the spirit of the Code as well as its letter' and that the impact of shareholders in monitoring the Code could be enhanced by better interaction between the boards of listed companies and their shareholders. The revised code, renamed the UK Corporate Governance Code, was published in June 2010. It encouraged the chairman to report personally in his or her annual statements on how the principles relating to the role and effectiveness of the board have been applied. It also recommended that, in the interests of greater accountability, all directors of FTSE 350 companies should be subject to annual re-election.

The major changes to the UK Corporate Governance Code between 2010 and 2016 are as follows.

MAJOR CHANGES IN UK CORPORATE GOVERNANCE CODE, 2012–16

- Organisations are required to provide information about risks that affect the longer-term viability of the organisation. Investors should assess the statements given by organisations on solvency, liquidity, risk management and viability, and engage accordingly.
- Organisations are required to include within service contracts provisions that will enable performance adjustment or post-vesting clawback for executive directors' variable pay (bonuses and long-term incentives), and specify the circumstances in which remuneration committees would consider it appropriate to act by retrieving money paid out to the director under one of these variable pay mechanisms. Remuneration committees

---

are faced with some difficult decisions relating to issues such as trigger events for clawback, how long the clawback risk should last, how to structure variable deferred pay to ensure ability to withhold or recover sums in practice, and managing shareholder expectations.

- Remuneration committees are responsible for ensuring that remuneration policies must be designed to deliver long-term benefit to the company. Performance-related elements of pay should be transparent and not encourage excessive risk taking.
- Boards are obliged, where a significant proportion of votes have been cast against or withheld on any resolution, to try to understand the reasons for the shareholders opposing it. They also need to explain how they intend to engage with shareholders in order to address their concerns.
- Boards should avoid 'group-think' and the Code suggests a way to do this is to introduce diversity on to the board. This diversity should consist of not just race and gender, but also skills and experience.
- Boards should set the right 'tone at the top' – culture, values and ethics – and lead by example.
- Chairs should report in annual statements on how the principles in Schedule A and B to the Code have been applied by the company. Schedule A relates to executive directors' performance-related pay and Schedule B covers the corporate governance arrangements of the company.

Changes to the UK Corporate Governance Code 2018

The revised UK Corporate Governance Code 2018 refocuses UK corporate governance on to the application of principles of best practice. It retains the 'comply and explain' regime. The Code sets out good practices to enable boards to:

- establish their company's purpose, strategy and values, and satisfy themselves that these are aligned to their company's culture and aimed at achieving long-term success for the company;
- consider the practices and processes that need to be put in place to ensure an effective interaction with the company's employees, customers, suppliers and wider stakeholders;
- develop effective policies to ensure diversity (gender, social and ethnic backgrounds, cognitive and personal strengths) on the board, within the management team and in the management pipeline; and

- ensure that appointments to boards are based on merit and objective criteria to avoid group think.

The Code includes new requirements for boards to consider the needs and views of a wider range of stakeholders, integrity and corporate culture, diversity and how the overall governance of the company contributes to its long-term success.

UK Stewardship Code

Corporate governance best practices states that there should be open communications between a company and its shareholders. The UK Stewardship Code, which was published in 2010 and revised in 2012 by the FRC, sets out the responsibilities of the institutional shareholders in this relationship. The company's responsibilities are set out in the UK Corporate Governance Code. It is a Code for institutional investors who are shareowners or who manage shareholdings for other financial institutions such as pension companies. Its aim is to encourage greater engagement between companies and their investors, so that the investors contribute positively to the governance of the companies in which they invest. The seven principles of the UK Stewardship Code are as follows.

THE SEVEN PRINCIPLES OF THE UK STEWARDSHIP CODE

Principle 1: Institutional investors should publicly disclose their policy on how they will discharge their stewardship responsibilities.

Principle 2: Institutional investors should have a robust policy on managing conflicts of interest in relation to stewardship, which should be publicly disclosed.

Principle 3: Institutional investors should monitor their investee companies.

Principle 4: Institutional investors should establish clear guidelines on when and how they will escalate their stewardship activities, i.e. escalate shareholder activism.

Principle 5: Institutional shareholders should be willing to act collectively with other investors where appropriate.

Principle 6: Institutional investors should have a clear policy on voting and disclosure of voting activity.

Principle 7: Institutional investors should report periodically on their stewardship and voting activities.

The Davies Report: Women on Boards

The UK Government asked Lord Davis to review the current status of women on the boards of the UK's largest companies. Lord Davis' conclusions were published in a report in 2011. It concluded that there was a case for a greater proportion of women on the boards of UK companies, there being only 12.5% female board members on FTSE 100 companies in 2010, as there was evidence that boards with greater diversity were 'more likely to be effective boards, better able to understand their customers and stakeholders, and to benefit fresh perspectives, vigorous challenge and broad experience. These in turn lead to better decision-making.'

The specific recommendations of the Davis Report were as follows:

- By 2015, FTSE 100 companies should have a minimum of 25% female representation on their board. This was raised in 2016 by the Hampton-Alexander Report to 33% female representation on FTSE 350 boards by 2020.
- Listed companies should disclose each year the proportion of women on their board, in senior executive positions and for the company as a whole.
- Listed companies should also establish, and report progress on each year, a policy for board room diversity, including measurable policy objectives. The report should include 'meaningful information' on how the nomination committee addressed the issue of diversity in its appointment process for board members.
- Companies should consider advertising for board members, as this may result in a more diverse pool of applicants.
- A voluntary code of conduct for executive search consultants should be developed to address gender diversity and best practices in searching for and nominating more diverse board members in FTSE 350 companies.

The Report rejected the previously held view that a director should be financially literate and have experience of financial responsibilities prior to becoming a director. It was felt that these could be learnt.

Hampton-Alexander Report

The Hampton-Alexander review was established in February 2016 to continue the work of Lord Davis. Its remit was to improve representation of women on FTSE 350 boards and to consider options for increasing the number of women in the executive layer of FTSE 350 companies, thus building a talent pipeline. The Report was published in November 2016. In addition to raising the target for women on boards mentioned above, the Report made recommendations for amendments to the UK Corporate Governance Code. These proposed amendments were included in the 2018 version of the Code.

2013 Executive Pay Reforms

The executive pay reforms that were introduced by the UK government in 2013 introduced new shareholder controls and oversight over executive remuneration in 'quoted companies', as defined in section 365 of the Companies Act 2006.

The main changes introduced by the executive pay reforms were as follows:

- The directors' remuneration report of listed companies should contain:
  - a statement by the chairman of the remuneration committee;
  - the company's policy on directors' remuneration; and
  - an implementation report, containing information on how the remuneration policy was implemented during the financial year.
- Shareholders have the right to vote on the remuneration policy as follows:
  - 'binding vote' on an ordinary resolution to approve the policy or any amendments to an existing shareholder approved policy. The remuneration policy should be placed before shareholders at least every three years; and
  - If the policy is rejected, a revised policy can be put to the vote of shareholders at another general meeting or the company could continue to use its existing policy.
- Shareholders have the right to vote on the implementation report annually, at the annual general meeting. This vote is an advisory vote only. If shareholders vote against an implementation report, then the company is required to put the remuneration policy to the shareholders at the next annual general meeting.
- If payments are made to board members that are inconsistent with the policy, the company can bring legal action against the board members who authorised the payment for its recovery.

EU Audit Regulations 2014

In 2014, the EU introduced new Audit Directive and Regulations which came into force in the UK from June 2016. The regulations applied to listed companies and included, among other things, requirements for non-audit work and audit firm rotation.

Non-audit work
The regulations:
- restrict the amount of non-audit work that audit firms can carry out for a client to no more than 70% of the average fees from the audit work over the previous three financial years; and
- impose a ban on certain types of non-audit work, such as work relating to design and implementation of financial internal controls, tax advice and book-keeping.

Audit firm rotation
The UK implementation of the regulations requires listed companies to change their audit firm at least every 20 years, with a ten-year retendering period.

2016 FRC Corporate Culture and the Role of Boards: Report of Observations

The FRC Corporate Culture Report was published in July 2016. It recognises that rules and sanctions on their own cannot deliver 'productive behaviours over the long-term'. Corporate culture is increasingly important in delivering long-term business and economic success. The report aimed 'to stimulate thinking around the role of the board in relation to culture and to encourage boards to reflect on what they were currently doing' with regard to culture in their organisations.

The Report highlights the following key observations on corporate culture:
- Recognise the value of culture.
- Demonstrate leadership.
- Be open and accountable.
- Embed and integrate.
- Assess, measure and engage.

- Align values.
- Exercise stewardship.

2016 Parker Report into Ethnic Diversity of UK Boards

The Parker Report, published in November 2016, concluded that listed companies in the UK did not reflect 'the ethnic diversity of either the UK or the stakeholders they seek to engage and represent'. The Report made three recommendations:
1. Increase ethnic diversity of UK boards.
2. Develop candidates for the pipeline and plan for succession.
3. Enhance transparency and disclosure.

Other sector codes

The UK Corporate Governance Code applies primarily to listed companies. However, other organisations within the UK have taken many of the best practices recommended by it and applied them. For example:
- in 1995 the Nolan Committee published the 'Seven Principles of Public Life' which apply to Members of Parliament, the civil service, non-departmental public bodies and the National Health Service. Nolan's Seven Principles have been amended over the years. Their current wording from 2015 is set out on page 59.
- The Good Governance Code: A Code for the Voluntary and Community Sector was published in the UK in 2005 and revised in 2010 and in 2017. The Code is now called the Charity Governance Code, and contains seven principles which set out how the boards of voluntary and community organisations should provide good governance and leadership:
Principle 1: Organisational purpose
Principle 2: Leadership
Principle 3: Integrity
Principle 4: Decision-making, risk and control
Principle 5: Board effectiveness
Principle 6: Diversity
Principle 7: Openness and accountability.
- The Corporate Governance Code and Guidance for Unlisted Companies was published in 2010 by the UK Institute of Directors (IoD) together with the European Conference of Directors'

Associations. The Code is voluntary. Its aim is to help ensure the long-term survival and sustainability of the company during its life cycle as it makes the transition from entrepreneurial leadership to a more professionally governed organisation. With this in mind, the Code is divided into two phases:
- phase 1: universal principles that apply to all unlisted companies
- phase 2: principles which apply to large and/or more complex companies.

NOLAN'S SEVEN PRINCIPLES OF PUBLIC LIFE

Principle 1: Selflessness – Holders of public office should act solely in terms of the public interest.

Principle 2: Integrity – Holders of public office must avoid placing themselves under any obligation to people or organisations that might try inappropriately to influence them in their work. They should not act or take decisions to gain financial or other material benefits for themselves, their family, or their friends. They must declare and resolve any interests and relationships.

Principle 3: Objectivity – Holders of public office must act and take decisions impartially, fairly and on merit, using the best evidence and without discrimination or bias.

Principle 4: Accountability – Holders of public office are accountable to the public for their decisions and actions, and must submit themselves to the scrutiny necessary to ensure this.

Principle 5: Openness – Holders of public office should act and take decisions in an open and transparent manner. Information should not be withheld from the public unless there are clear and lawful reasons for so doing.

Principle 6: Honesty – Holders of public office should be truthful.

Principle 7: Leadership – Holders of public office should exhibit these principles in their own behaviour. They should actively promote and robustly support the principles, and be willing to challenge poor behaviour wherever it occurs.

South African corporate governance

The King Reports

In November 1994, the Institute of Directors of Southern Africa published the first King Report, in response to the development of South Africa's stock market. The first King Report has now been superseded by the second King Report (King II), which was published in March 2002, the third King Report (King III) published in September 2009 and the fourth King Report (King IV) published in November 2016.

As in the UK, the first two King Reports adopted the 'comply or explain' approach to corporate governance. King III, however, adopted the 'apply or explain' approach because the authors believed that the code should be applied on a non-legislated basis. The King Reports also differ from the UK approach as they adopt the 'inclusive approach' to corporate governance described in Chapter 1.

King III defines corporate governance in terms of leadership sustainability and good corporate citizenship. It incorporates many emerging corporate governance trends such as alternative dispute resolution and risk-based internal audit, as well as introducing new issues such as information technology governance and business rescue. Through integrated reporting, King III requires companies to report on how their activities impact (both positively and negatively) on the economic life of the communities in which they operate, and how the company intends to enhance the positive aspects and eradicate or lessen the negative aspects in the future. It also applies to all entities in South Africa regardless of the manner and form of incorporation or establishment and whether they are in the public, private or not-for-profit sectors.

King IV builds on King III. As mentioned above, King III adopted an 'apply or explain' approach to disclosure. King IV introduces an 'apply and explain'. There is an assumed application of the principles in King IV. The disclosure is an explanation on the practices that have been implemented and how these support achieving the associated governance principle. The governing body can choose where and how to make the disclosures which should be publicly accessible.

King IV also aligns best practices in corporate governance to shifts in the approaches to:

- capitalism – financial capital to inclusive capital market systems;
- reporting – 'silo' i.e. by capital e.g. financial, human etc. to 'integrated' reporting; and
- capital markets – short-term to sustainable capital markets.

The focus of King IV is on outcomes-based governance. It places accountability on the governing body within an organisation to attain four governance outcomes:

- ethical culture and effective leadership;
- performance and value creation in a sustainable manner;
- adequate and effective controls; and
- trust, good reputation and legitimacy with stakeholders.

King VI introduces a principle applicable to institutional investors.

The King Reports have repositioned corporate governance in Africa as a method of achieving sustainability of organisations rather than just a method of protecting investors. They have also integrated good citizenship and ethics into the thematic area of corporate governance, something seen as essential in a region struggling with issues such as corruption and health and skills development.

The approach in the King Reports is being emulated in legislation and code development throughout the region as it is seen as more appropriate for the needs of countries and organisations. It is hoped that through this repositioning, more organisations will see the appropriateness of corporate governance to their sustainability with the consequential economic development it should produce.

Companies Act 71 of 2008

The Companies Act 71 of 2008 (CA2008) came into force in May 2011 and applies to all South African companies. It was a total rewrite of previous company law provisions. Its aim was to improve corporate governance in South Africa.

The CA2008 brought into law many of the corporate governance principles that had been institutionalised in South Africa by the King Reports I and II. These include sections on:

- corporate leadership;
- transparency and accountability;
- codification of certain directors' duties;
- company secretary residency in South Africa;
- corporate responsibility;
- stakeholder protection;
- shareholder rights and powers; and
- protection for minority shareholders.

Johannesburg Stock Exchange (JSE) Listing Requirements

The JSE Listing Requirements require all listed companies to provide in their annual reports a statement on how they have applied the principles set out in King, together with an explanation which enables shareholders to evaluate how the principles have been applied. Where principles have not been applied, the listed company is required to provide a statement in their annual report setting out the reasons for the non-compliance.

Since April 2010, the JSE Listing Requirements have imposed on listed companies the following mandatory requirements:

- A separate chief executive officer and an independent non-executive chairman. If the chairman is not independent, then a lead independent director should be appointed.
- Policies setting out:
  - the formal and transparent appointment process for all board members;
  - the balance of power and authority at board level; and
  - details on non-audit services provided by external auditors.
- The majority of the members of the nominations committee must be independent, with a minimum membership of two non-executive directors. The nomination committee should be chaired by the chairman.
- Audit and remuneration committees should be established. In their annual reports, listed companies should disclose the composition of these committees and any other board committees with a brief description of all committee mandates, meetings held by the committees in the year of reporting and any other relevant information.
- CVs of all directors standing for election or re-election must accompany the notice of the annual general meeting.
- Each director must be categorised as an executive director, non-executive director or independent director.

G20/OECD Corporate Governance Principles

In 1999, the Organisation for Economic Co-operation and Development (OECD)), which monitors developments in corporate governance in member countries, published a set of principles of good governance.

These principles were revised in 2004 and 2015.

The OECD principles became known as the G20/OECD Corporate Governance Principles when they were endorsed by the G20 leaders in November 2015. According to the OECD, the principles were revised 'to address the challenges of increasing complexity of the investment chain, the changing role of stock exchanges and the emergence of new investors, investment strategies and trading practices'.

The G20/OECD principles are divided into six sections, covering:

1. ensuring the basis for an effective corporate governance framework;
2. the rights of shareholders;
3. the equitable treatment of shareholders;
4. the role of stakeholders;
5. disclosure and transparency; and
6. the responsibilities of the board.

The purpose of the principles was to help governments in their efforts to improve the legal institutional and regulatory framework for corporate governance in their countries. They were also intended to provide a source of suggestions and guidance for stock exchanges, institutions, companies and other organisations that had a role to play in instigating good governance practices. The principles provide a benchmark for good governance for organisation such as the World Bank and for non-member countries.

In addition to the Corporate Governance Principles, the OECD has also published guidelines for multinationals on how they should run their foreign subsidiaries, guidelines for state-owned industries and guidelines on the problem of bribery as a corporate practice in some emerging markets.

The rest of the world

Corporate governance scandals are unfortunately happening all around the world. In Japan, two of the best-known brands, Mitsubishi Motors and Olympus Corporation, have suffered scandals in recent years:

- The car manufacturer Mitsubishi Motors admitted in April 2016 that it had been inflating the fuel efficiency of a number of its models of cars since 2002. The revelation led to a fall in sales and the company's stock price.

- In 2011, the CEO of Olympus Corporation, Michael Woodford, was ousted following his revelation that Olympus had been hiding losses since the 1980s. The scandal led to press speculation that Olympus was connected to the Yakuza Japanese, (an organised crime syndicate), which Olympus denied. The scandal wiped around 75% off the price of shares and led to the resignation of most of the board.

In Australia, the Australia and New Zealand Banking Group has also suffered from a number of scandals. The most recent was in 2016 when legal proceedings were brought against ANZ and ten of its traders for manipulating the benchmark interbank interest rates in Australia, and attempting cartel conduct relating to the manipulation of the Malaysian ringgit.

At the time of writing, some 98 countries around the world have corporate governance codes or regulations. There are also a plethora of international and regional codes and standards. The European Corporate Governance Institute (ECGI) has on its website an 'Index of Codes' which includes, in many cases, copies of the codes of best practice.

Chapter summary

- Corporate malpractice is not new; it has been around for as long as corporations have existed.
- Corporate governance best practice started to develop in the early 1990s in the UK, in reaction to certain corporate governance scandals.
- Other countries have adopted corporate governance best practices, and in some cases have adapted them to their own specific requirements.
- At the time of writing, 98 countries have codes or regulations on corporate governance.

4   Corporate governance players

Introduction

It is often stated that the board of directors/leadership of an organisation is responsible for governance. However, in all organisations, there are other players who contribute to the overall governance of the organisation. This chapter discusses the roles of shareholders, board of directors, company secretary, governance officer and management/executive in the governance of organisations.

The owners/founders/shareholders

The governance implications of ownership

Discussions about ownership/shareholding of organisations tend to focus on ownership structures and the governance implications as well as legal and regulatory frameworks governing ownership/shareholder rights. The issues of concern vary depending on the nature of the organisation. In family businesses, the issues relate to participation rights and measures to ensure smooth transition from the founders to the next generation. In private companies, the issues include roles of controlling shareholders and protection of minority shareholders. In large public listed companies, the ownership issues largely relate to the agency problem that arises from separation of ownership and control, and measures to mitigate the agency problem, such as the effectiveness of monitoring and bonding mechanisms. The former include internal controls, risk management and reporting mechanisms as well as the audit function. The latter include compensation and remuneration arrangements.

Primary governance functions of shareholders

In most commercial organisations such as companies, shareholders are those who contribute equity capital. In other organisations such as associations, charities and trusts, ownership or status equivalent to shareholders is vested in members, founders and settlors. They determine the objects/purpose of the organisation, mobilise resources for the organisation and appoint key staff, including the governing bodies. These are the roles most often cited for owners/founders/shareholders. However, they also have governance responsibilities.

Owners/founders/shareholders have the primary responsibility to determine the governance framework for the organisation.

The UK Corporate Governance Code 2018 in its introduction makes an important point about the role of shareholders in governance. The code goes beyond basic ownership functions and places the primary responsibility for governance structures on the owners.

> The shareholders' role in governance is to appoint the directors and the auditors and to satisfy themselves that an appropriate governance structure is in place.

UK Corporate Governance Code, 2018

Therefore, in all organisations, including charities, family businesses and private companies, owners/founders/shareholders need to ensure that there are appropriate governance structures and arrangements. This includes determining the nature and structure of governance organs, and clarifying the roles and responsibilities of each organ. While companies have three levels of governance (the shareholders, the board and management), most organisations such as trusts, charities and foundations have two levels of governance: the board or equivalent oversight body and management.

Key ownership functions and governance

Shareholders invest capital into a company by way of equity. Legal frameworks such as company law provide for key ownership functions that include, for example, determining the objects and purpose of the organisation, and appointing the board of directors. In companies, key ownership functions include determining the objects and purpose of the company, appointing the board of directors (subject to regulatory requirements), appointing auditors, approving a dividend proposed by the directors, and approving major transactions such as mergers and acquisitions. These functions have implications for governance, as outlined below.

Objects and purpose of an organisation

Owners/founders/shareholders determine the objects and purpose of an organisation. Although the objects and purpose are no longer required to be stated in the formation documents such as the Memorandum of Association, they enable an organisation to articulate what it seeks to achieve. In addition, the organisation's core values and strategy must be aligned with the objects and purpose. Chapter 6 deals with creating an ethical culture and explains the role of the board in ensuring that the core values of the organisation are aligned with its vision, mission and strategy. This ensures alignment of the owners and managers, thus mitigating some of the factors that contribute to unethical conduct such as investor/shareholder expectations.

Governance and finance

The link between governance and finance is twofold. First, providers of capital, particularly equity finance, have a key role to play in determining the governance of an organisation. This also applies those who establish other types of organisations, such as charities and trusts. Second, the empirical research has demonstrated a link between governance and finance. This is particularly where organisations seek to raise external finance. Good governance is critical for both debt and equity finance, and the basic principles of corporate governance – accountability, fairness and transparency – are central to both issues.

The board of directors

As stated above, the owners/shareholders/founders determine the objects and purpose of an organisation. They appoint a board of directors whose role has evolved from a narrow concept of what the board is responsible for – that is, management of the business of the organisation – to a role that combines both entrepreneurial leadership and governance. The board is accountable to shareholders and stakeholders for both the 'what' and 'how'.

- **What** has the organisation achieved in terms of its purpose?
- **How** has the organisation achieved its purpose?

The audit function

The audit function is a monitoring mechanism that assures owners/founders/shareholders who are not in control that the information provided by those in control is accurate and reliable. This aids decision-making for both shareholders and stakeholders such as investors and regulators. It supports the key governance principles of transparency and accountability.

The AGM and governance

The annual general meeting (AGM) is the forum where shareholders exercise their governance responsibilities including appointing directors, appointing auditors and approving the dividend proposed by shareholders. Corporate governance standards require organisations to adopt measures that empower shareholders to effectively participate at AGMs including providing full and accurate information, allowing shareholders to seek clarification and ask questions, and communication by electronic means, as well as voting by proxy and in absentia.

Regulation of ownership

Increasingly, organisations/companies that operate in regulated sectors such as financial institutions are subject to legal and regulatory frameworks have an impact ownership, such as restrictions on acquiring or increasing controls. The Financial Services and Markets Act 2000 (Controllers) Regulations 2009 contain provisions on acquiring or increasing control and changes in holding of a UK authorised person. This is a person authorised under the Financial Services and Markets Act 2000 to carry on one or more authorised activities. Acquiring control is defined in section 181 to mean acquiring 10% or more of shares or voting power or significant influence over the management of an organisation. Reducing or ceasing to have control means ceasing to have 10% or more control or voting power or significant influence over the management of an organisation.

Relations with owners

Strained relations with owners can cause wide ranging problems for companies including acrimonious AGMs, bad publicity, proxy fights and mistrust. Constructive dialogue with owners/founders/shareholders enables the board to have an understanding of the views or issues of concern as well as ensure alignment on strategy and governance.

The UK Corporate Governance Code 2018 places responsibility for relations with shareholders on the board chairman and committee chairs.

The chairman is required to ensure satisfactory dialogue with major shareholders and that the board has a full understanding of the views and concerns of shareholders.

Ownership rights and governance

Regardless of the organisation, there are key principles that should be observed in relation to ownership and the G20/OECD Principles aptly reflect this in Principle II below.

G20/OECD Principles of Corporate Governance

II. The rights and equitable treatment of shareholders and key ownership functions

The corporate governance framework should protect and facilitate the exercise of shareholders' rights and ensure the equitable treatment of all shareholders, including minority and foreign shareholders. All shareholders should have the opportunity to obtain effective redress for violation of their rights.

The treatment of shareholders and the extent to which they are able to exercise their rights has implications for governance and finance. Both internal and external governance frameworks determine the nature and scope of participation by shareholders. External governance frameworks such as company law and other forms of organisational law provide for mechanisms of establishing ownership, participation rights, governance structures and accountability frameworks. Internally, measures to ensure effective shareholder participation in governance include clarifying the roles and responsibilities of all governance organs, ensuring timely and reliable disclosure of information, and adopting measures to enable shareholders to exercise their voice and interact such as voting in absentia by mail or electronic means. In addition, measures that allow for frequent interaction and communication between shareholders such as shareholder associations and online forums enhance the participation of shareholders, particularly for organisations where ownership is dispersed.

Secure methods of ownership

In all organisations, it is important to have a framework that governs ownership of the entities. In most jurisdictions, this will be the law that establishes those organisations, such as company law which not only provides for methods of incorporating companies, but provisions on ownership registration as well. These include provisions on subscribing to the memorandum and articles, the obligation to keep a share register and provisions on transfer and transmission of shares. These provisions provide the mechanisms for ascertaining and verifying ownership, the basis for exercising ownership rights, including participation and information rights. Part A of Principle II of the G20/OECD Corporate Governance Principles provides the general scope of ownership rights.

G20/OECD Principles of Corporate Governance

II. The rights and equitable treatment of shareholders and key ownership functions

A. Basic shareholder rights should include the right to: 1) secure methods of ownership registration; 2) convey or transfer shares; 3) obtain relevant and material information on the corporation on a timely and regular basis; 4) participate and vote in general shareholder meetings; 5) elect and remove members of the board; and 6) share in the profits of the corporation.

Clarity of participation rights

Flowing from ownership rights are participation rights. The issue is: once ownership has been ascertained, what are the rights of those owners? How are decisions made and how do the owners relate to each other? Organisational law (the various laws that govern incorporation/establishment of organisations such as company law, trust law, laws governing the establishment of charitable organisations and others) provides the framework for participation rights and these include rights to vote, appoint a board of directors, appoint auditors and approve a dividend, among others. The manner in which these rights are exercised is also important. Therefore, issues such as access to information to aid decision-making, voting by proxy and in absentia, and ability to consult and exercise voice are critical.

Most legal frameworks provide for voting by proxy and procedural requirements for placing items on the agenda of shareholder meetings, particularly the AGM.

Other measures that encourage shareholder participation include voting by mail, shareholder consultative forums using social media and other online platforms, and access to information via email and other electronic means. Organisations are also increasingly allowing shareholders to exercise their voice on matters such as remuneration.

Media reports of AGM meetings show that shareholders are increasingly able to use AGMs to express their views on key matters such as executive remuneration, falling share prices and litigation expenses. This is in line with Principle D of the UK Corporate Governance Code 2018, which states that in order for the company to meet its responsibilities to shareholders, there should be effective engagement and participation from shareholders and stakeholders. The Code, as stated previously, places the responsibility for meaningful dialogue with shareholders primarily on the board chair and requires directors to be informed about major shareholder issues and concerns.

Principle II of the G20/OECD Corporate Governance outlines the general framework for participation including:

- sufficient and timely information for meetings;
- removal of barriers to participation in meetings;
- exercise of voice by shareholders including asking questions, placing items on the agenda and giving their views on issues such as remuneration and appointment of directors;
- ability to vote in absentia; and
- measures to remove obstacles to cross border voting.

Information rights

Shareholders/founders/owners may be involved in the day-to-day management of the organisation or may not, as is the case with most shareholders in large public listed companies. The former have access to information by virtue of their participation in the management of the company. However, the latter require frameworks that ensure access to accurate and reliable information. This includes financial information, material information on matters such as acquisitions and mergers, related party transactions, interests of directors and risk factors.

Access to information aids decision making as well as ensues that those exercising control are accountable to those who are not involved in the day-to-day management of the organisation. Accountability is a key principle of corporate governance and the UK Corporate Governance Code 2018 presents the principle in the context of financial and business reporting. It places the responsibility on the board to present a fair, balanced and understandable assessment of the company's position and prospects.

Access to reliable and accurate information is critical for those not involved in the day-to-day management of the organisation as well as for decision making. Stock market regulations and other regulatory standards prescribe time frames for disclosure of financial information such as interim and final accounts. Financial reporting standards provide the framework for disclosure of financial information. However, organisations need to go beyond financial reporting. As stated in the UK Corporate Governance Code 2018, directors need to provide the information necessary for shareholders to assess the company's position, performance, business model and strategy over the longer term. These requirements enable shareholders and other stakeholders to have a broader view of the affairs of an organisation.

Equitable treatment

Corporate governance frameworks recognise variations in ownership structures. Most organisations have retail, institutional, majority and minority shareholders. The key issues of concern are treatment of minority shareholders, the role of institutional shareholders and measures to avoid conflicts of interest by ensuring transparency and arm's-length relationships. While the UK Corporate Governance Code 2018 Code emphasises the need to maintain dialogue with and engage with major shareholders, it is important to treat all shareholders fairly and equitably. Organisations should have mechanisms to prevent abusive and manipulative conduct by outsiders such as insider dealing and market manipulation, as well as having policies and measures to manage conflicts of interest involving insiders and controlling owners.

The board of directors/leadership of an organisation

What is the role of the board?

The narrow perspective – company law

The directors of a company/organisation are appointed by the shareholders, and legal frameworks such as company law provide in very general terms that the role of the directors is to manage the affairs of the company. However, this mandate is very broad and not clarified in legal frameworks.

It is important to understand historical perspectives of the role of the board and how these have evolved over time. Article 3 of the Companies (Model Articles) Regulations 2008 provides that subject to the Articles, the directors are responsible for the management of the company's business, for which purpose they may exercise all the powers of the company. The role of the board has been historically stated as such in company legislation in the UK and various parts of the world. The use of the term 'management' is interesting, as corporate governance experts including Bob Tricker (corporate governance expert and author of one of the first books on the subject, *International Corporate Governance: Text, Readings and Cases*, published in 1994) say there is a difference between management and governance.

The broader perspective — the UK Corporate Governance Code 2018

Corporate governance standards articulate the role of the board more broadly than company legislation. According to the Code, the function of the board is 'to promote the long-term sustainable success of the company, generate value for shareholders and contribute to wider society'. The board should also ensure that 'the necessary resources are in place for the company to meet its objectives and measure performance against them', and should also establish effective systems of internal control and risk management.

The broader perspective — the OECD Principles

> The corporate governance framework should ensure the strategic guidance of the company, the effective monitoring of management by the board, and the board's accountability to the company and the shareholders.
>
> (G20/OECD Principles of Corporate Governance, p.51)

Corporate governance codes and standards have helped to clarify the role of the board of directors. The responsibilities of the board are aptly summarised in the following excerpt from the G20/OCED Principles of Corporate Governance:

> Together with guiding corporate strategy, the board is chiefly responsible for monitoring managerial performance and achieving an adequate return for shareholders, while preventing conflicts of interest and balancing competing demands on the corporation. In order for boards to effectively fulfil their responsibilities, they must be able to exercise objective and independent judgement. Another important board responsibility is to oversee the risk management system and systems designed to ensure that the corporation obeys

applicable laws, including tax, competition, labour, environmental, equal opportunity, health and safety laws. In some countries, companies have found it useful to explicitly articulate the responsibilities that the board assumes and those for which management is accountable.

The board and leadership

Some corporate governance codes provide detailed roles and responsibilities of the board of directors while others, such as the UK Corporate Governance Code 2018, focus on key aspects in relation to the board such as leadership, composition and performance. The Code states that every company should be headed by an effective and entrepreneurial board which is collectively responsible for the long-term success of the company, generating value for shareholders and contributing to the wider society. It further states that as part of their role as members of a unitary board, non-executive directors should provide constructive challenge and strategic guidance, offer specialist advice and hold management to account.

There are four aspects that need to be unpacked from the principle on leadership, as follows:

1. Effectiveness – the Code provides guidance on effectiveness where various factors that contribute to board effectiveness are outlined including board and committee composition and skills, appointment procedures, commitment, induction and training, access to information and performance evaluation.

2. Responsibility for long-term success – this is reflected in various principles including accountability, where the board is required to go beyond financial reporting and demonstrate how the company generates or preserves value over the long term. It is also in line with other corporate governance principles and theories such as sustainability and stakeholder relations. Both require organisations to ensure that their operations and activities are sustainable and take into account the legitimate needs and expectations of key stakeholders.

3. Constructive challenge – the board is expected to challenge management constructively on key issues such as strategy formulation. Doing this requires a competent board with diverse skills

with a deep understanding of the organisation and the environment in which it operates.

4. Strategy development – a key role of the board is to provide strategic direction for the organisation. The board is expected to provide guidance to management on key strategic objectives taking into account short-, medium- and long-term perspectives, risks, opportunities and available resources.

The roles and responsibilities of the board in the UK Corporate Governance Code 2018, the G20/OECD Corporate Governance Principles and South Africa's King IV Code are compared below.

G20/OECD Principles of Corporate Governance

D. The board should fulfil certain key functions, including:

1. Reviewing and guiding corporate strategy, major plans of action, risk management policies and procedures, annual budgets and business plans; setting performance objectives; monitoring implementation and corporate performance; and overseeing major capital expenditures, acquisitions and divestitures.

2. Monitoring the effectiveness of the company's governance practices and making changes as needed.

3. Selecting, compensating, monitoring and, when necessary, replacing key executives and overseeing succession planning.

4. Aligning key executive and board remuneration with the longer term interests of the company and its shareholders.

5. Ensuring a formal and transparent board nomination and election process.

6. Monitoring and managing potential conflicts of interest of management, board members and shareholders, including misuse of corporate assets and abuse in related party transactions.

7. Ensuring the integrity of the corporation's accounting and financial reporting systems, including the independent audit, and that appropriate systems of control are in place, in particular, systems for risk management, financial and operational control, and compliance with the law and relevant standards.

8. Overseeing the process of disclosure and communications.

The King IV Code of Corporate Governance for South Africa, 2016

3.1 Role of the governing body

The governing body should serve as the focal point and custodian of corporate governance in the organization.

Recommended practices

The governing body should serve as the focal point and custodian of corporate governance in the organization. This broad leadership role includes:

a. Providing direction and strategy
b. Giving effect to strategy by approving policy including plans, frameworks, structures and procedures
c. Providing oversight of implementation, and
d. Demonstrating accountability and transparency through disclosure

The board of directors is critical to the overall governance framework of an organisation, and as such, issues relating to appointment, composition and structure of the board, board leadership, performance and remuneration are some factors that have a direct bearing on ability to deliver on its mandate.

The appointment of directors

Organisations should have clear and transparent processes for appointment of directors. This should be guided by the nature of the organisation and skills and competencies required to achieve the organisation's objectives. Key considerations in the appointment of directors include transparency, the role of the board and shareholders, and the need to refresh the board periodically.

Appointment of directors is a process that involves various stakeholders. A board may be composed of executive and non-executive directors. The former are usually full time employees of an organisation such as the Chief Executive Officer (CEO), the Finance Director or Chief Finance Officer (CFO) or other officers of the organisation. These individuals are part of the senior management team and are directors by virtue of their primary appointments. Non-executive directors may be independent or represent major shareholders. Various parties are involved in the appointment of non-executive directors, including the board of directors, regulators and shareholders. At board level, the nominations committee of the board is usually charged with the responsibility of periodically reviewing the skills and competencies of the board to identify gaps as well as identify potential candidates for appointment to the board. The committee then makes recommendations to the board.

Regulatory bodies such as the Financial Conduct Authority (FCA) carry out fit and proper assessment for all persons carrying out controlled functions. According to the FCA, being a controlled person includes being a director of a regulated firm, overseeing the firm's systems and controls, and being responsible for compliance with the FCA's rules. The assessment covers honesty (openness with self-disclosures, integrity and reputation), competence and capability, and financial soundness. For dual regulated firms (those regulated by the FCA and Prudential Regulatory Authority, or PRA), fit and proper assessments of directors and CEOs are led by the PRA. The formal appointment of directors is made by shareholders at the AGM pursuant to the provisions of the Companies Act.

The involvement of various players in the appointment of directors requires clarity of roles of the various players. Historically, the appointment of directors was a shareholder function. However, diverse ownership structures and regulatory requirements have led to the emergence of other players. The responsibilities of the board are to review composition of the board periodically vis-à-vis skills required for the board to execute its responsibilities effectively. In addition, the board should have clear procedures for identifying and nominating directors. Shareholders participate at various levels. Major shareholders, including institutional shareholders, may have representatives on the board. At the AGM, the role of the shareholders is to approve the appointment of directors. This should not be a rubber-stamping exercise. Shareholders should be provided with information about candidates proposed for appointment. Table 4.1 provides an illustration of the roles of various players in the appointment of directors.

Transparency is key in the appointment of directors. The G20/0ECD Principles note that there are increasing calls for open search processes and that although procedures for appointing directors may differ across jurisdictions, it is the responsibility of the board to ensure that established processes for nomination and appointment of directors are observed. Where an organisation does not have established processes, the nominations committee should guide the board and develop criteria for nomination and appointment to the board.

Table 4.1: The roles of various players in the appointment of directors

Shareholders/AGM	The board	Regulators, e.g. FCA, PRA
• Approve remuneration of directors • Receive report on performance of directors • Approve appointment of directors • Receive particulars of persons nominated for appointment as directors	• Recommend directors for appointment to AGM • Nominations committee recommends to the board directors nominated for appointment • Nominations committee identifies suitable candidates for appointment to the board • Nominations committee periodically reviews board compositions and skills requirements	• Assess fitness and propriety of persons performing controlled functions • Receive applications from firms for persons to be appointed as directors of those firms to be assessed for fitness and properness

Potential directors need to understand the time and commitment required to perform their duties and responsibilities effectively. This should be communicated during the selection process so that potential directors are aware of what is expected of them. The selection process requires taking into account other directorships held by the nominee director.

Following appointment of new directors, orientation and induction should be arranged to enable them to understand the business of the organisation.

Irrespective of the nature of organisation and ownership structure, board composition is critical for board effectiveness. Diversity of skills and competencies is a key factor and has for a long time been the focus of discussions on board composition. For over a decade, Europe has spearheaded the discourse on gender diversity, with some jurisdictions such as Norway introducing quotas. A 2016 study on gender quotas revealed divergent views. In a study involving over 300 companies in Europe and the USA, it was established that there were negative attitudes towards quotas in countries that did not have them. In addition, countries with quotas had registered increased diversity and improved director selection processes (Wiersema and Mors, 2016). The G20/OECD Principles advocate for an inclusive approach to governance that recognises the need for various stakeholders to participate in corporate wealth creation.

Some leading corporations have in recent years received criticism and faced pressure from investors to diversify their governing bodies and senior leadership. For example in 2016, the Board of Apple Incorporated, whose core values include inclusion and diversity, rejected calls for diversity as unduly burdensome and unnecessary; in March 2017, the shareholders overwhelmingly rejected a diversity proposal. Tesla founder and CEO Elon Musk has openly disagreed with investors who want to see a more independent board.

The following statement from the Ford Foundation illustrates the link between independence and diversity.

> Foundation trustees bring a vast range of knowledge and experience to the task of governing the foundation. Over the years, trustees have hailed from five continents, and they have extensive experience in the worlds of higher education, business, law, government, technology, health care, nonprofit management, the arts, and the civic sector.
>
> The Ford Foundation places high value on the independence of our board members. We require that a majority of our trustees be independent, that all trustees serving on the Audit Committee meet a heightened independence standard.

Structure and composition of the board

> The board and its committees should have a balance of skills, experience, independence and knowledge. Board membership should be regularly refreshed.
>
> (UK Corporate Governance Code 2018)

It is interesting to note that legal frameworks that provide for estab-lishment of organisations such as company law do not deal with issues of structure and composition of the board. Instead they simply prescribe statutory requirements such as the minimum number of directors, minimum age and other qualification requirements. Over time, it was realised that structure and composition impact the functioning and effectiveness of the governing body. Codes of corporate governance provide best practice standards on these aspects. In addition, legal, regulatory and corporate governance standards also prescribe requirements relating to structure and composition of the board.

Composition and structure have implications for board effectiveness. Organisations need to consider carefully the skills requirements for their governing bodies and review periodically the composition of the board in relation to skills and competencies. All organisations, whether commercial or charity, operate in a dynamic environment characterised by rapid changes in technology, customer needs and stakeholder expectations. To maintain a competitive edge and remain relevant, governing bodies need to have the necessary skills and competencies to provide strategic direction in a dynamic environment.

Committees contribute to board effectiveness and therefore it is important for the governing body to review periodically its committee structure in relation to the strategic objectives and business of the organisation. Committee leadership and composition should take into account the terms of reference for each committee and the skills required to execute their mandate effectively.

Leadership of the board – the board chairman

Corporate governance standards on the role of the chairman

The chair leads the board and is responsible for its overall effectiveness in directing the company.

(UK Corporate Governance Code 2018)

The chairman's primary role is to ensure that the board is effective in its tasks of setting and implementing the company's direction and strategy.

(Institute of Directors of Southern Africa)

The leadership of the board is critical to the effective functioning of the board. The key roles of the board chairman include:

- board leadership including board cohesiveness, dynamics and communication;

- board composition and structure including skill, diversity, committees among others;
- board functionality including meetings of the board and committees, access to information, board performance evaluation;
- board–management relationships;
- maintaining relationships with key stakeholders of the organisation; and
- mentor, coach and counsellor to the CEO.

Separation of the roles of the chairman and CEO

Most corporate governance codes advocate for separation of roles between the board chairman and chief executive. In some jurisdictions such as the United States, legal and regulatory frameworks do not prescribe separation of roles. However, there is evidence of an increasing trend towards separation of roles with nearly half of Standard & Poors 500 Index (S&P) companies reporting split roles. Companies with dual roles appoint a lead independent director. In Europe, there is a clear trend of separation of roles. The UK Corporate Governance Code 2018 advocates for clear separation of roles between the chair, who leads the board and the chief executive officer who exercises executive responsibility for the company. The reasons for this are the need to ensure balance of power and avoid domination and reliance on a single individual. The King IV Code of South Africa is emphatic on the need to have an independent non-executive member as chair, to lead the governing body in the objective and effective discharge of its governance role and responsibilities.

The theoretical foundations for separation of roles is aptly summarised as follows:

> In theory, an independent chairman improves the ability of the board of directors to oversee management. By separating the positions, a company clearly differentiates between the roles of the board and management, and gives one director clear authority to speak on behalf of the board and to run board meetings. Separation eliminates conflicts in the areas of performance evaluation, executive compensation, succession planning, and the recruitment of new directors. It also allows the CEO to focus exclusively on strategy, operations, and organisational issues while the chairman

focuses on management oversight, board leadership, and governance-related matters.

(Larcker and Tayan, 2016)

It is important to be mindful that the position of board chairman is an increasingly demanding and visible role. Therefore, prior to appointing a chairman, it is important to establish other responsibilities and the ability of the potential candidate to effectively serve as chairman.

Key competencies of the chairman

Key competencies required of the chairman include:

- executive leadership (either as CEO or CFO);
- managerial experience;
- influencing skills;
- leadership; and
- ethics and integrity.

A study by Elise Walton identified three key prerequisites for an effective chairmanship. These are:

- the chemistry of the chair–CEO relationship characterised by frequent and open communication, and close but not personal relationship;
- a clear governance framework evidenced by clarity of roles, effective processes, leadership transition strategy); and
- an enabling context that includes a competent and supportive board, strong and accessible management team, and the right culture.

The lead independent director

The appointment of a lead independent director is now recognised as best practice by most corporate governance standards, particularly in cases where the roles of the chairman and chief executive are fused. The key responsibilities of the lead independent director include serving as a sounding board for the chairman as well as an intermediary for the other directors, leading the evaluation of the chairman, and serving as a point of call for the shareholders or other stakeholders in the event of difficult relations with the chairman.

Director remuneration

Compensation or remuneration is an important aspect of corporate governance. Remuneration of non-executive directors should be determined through a transparent process, taking into account their roles and responsibilities and time commitment required.

Non-executive director remuneration

The issue of director remuneration should be examined in the context in which a board operates or functions. Boards usually comprise both executive and non-executive directors. The former are employees of the organisation and their remuneration is part of the terms and conditions of their service. Non-executive directors are not full-time employees, and may be independent or represent major stakeholders such as shareholders. They have statutory duties and potential liability if they act in breach of those duties. The separation of ownership and control in large listed companies places significant responsibility on the board. Therefore, directors (both executive and non-executive) are expected not only to act in the best interests of the company, but also to devote sufficient time to the affairs of the company. Therefore, directors' remuneration should take into account their responsibilities and the manner in which a board functions. The following questions arise from this issue:

- How should directors be remunerated?
- Who determines the remuneration of directors?
- How does the governance framework assign responsibility for remuneration?

The governance of director remuneration

Both the board and shareholders have a role to play in director remuneration. At board level, director remuneration is part of the terms of reference of the remuneration committee. Most corporate governance standards require the committee to be chaired by an independent director and to have a majority of members as non-executive directors. This ensures independence and objectivity in determining the levels and structure of remuneration of the directors.

The committee makes a recommendation to the board, which then seeks approval of the shareholders. Board remuneration and any other benefits to directors are part of the disclosures required to be made

Remuneration committee
- Determine levels of remuneration for executive and non-executive directors
- Periodically review and benchmark remuneration

The board
- Remuneration policy and structures
- Disclosure of remuneration

Shareholders
- Right to be informed
- Approval of certain components of remuneration such as long-term incentive schemes in the case of listed companies
- Right to express views on remuneration

Figure 4.1: Director remuneration: the roles of the board and shareholders

annually. Figure 4.1 illustrates the roles and responsibilities of various parties with regard to director remuneration.

Executive director remuneration

Executive remuneration has various components including salary, bonuses, stock options, benefits and prerequisites. Globally, since the 1980s there has been an explosion in executive compensation and this was attributed to various factors including competition and a strong notion of a link between pay and performance. The level and structure of executive compensation have both generated controversy and intense debates and research. Although this is a board matter, it is evident that shareholders increasingly have the opportunity to express their views on executive compensation. In the UK, executive compensation is an ever more heated subject at AGMs, particularly in circumstances where investors are dissatisfied with performance.

To address weakness in pay structures, particularly incentive-based payments, the UK Corporate Governance Code 2018 requires performance-related elements of compensation to 'be clear, stretching, rigorously applied and aligned to the successful delivery of the strategy.' Transparency enables shareholders and investors to compare pay schemes and communicate their views and expectations. The requirement for schemes to be stretched and rigorously applied seeks to mitigate the negative practices or behaviour associated with performance-related payments, such as fraudulent accounting and mis-statements or other practices that conceal poor performance. Following the 2008 crisis, there is increased use of malus and claw- back clauses in executive compensation contracts. The former permit companies to withhold variable payments while the latter allows for ex-post recovery of payments linked to performance such as bonuses following a restatement of financial statements. There is wide support and voluntary adoption of clawback clauses which are considered as a tool to mitigate the incentives of misreporting. The UK Corporate Governance Code 2018 provides that remuneration schemes and policies include provisions to recover and/or withhold remuneration of cash or share awards, if performance is not satisfactory.

Board performance evaluation

The effective functioning of a board requires several measures. Some have been discussed above, including composition and the need to review and refresh the board periodically. Performance evaluation is another measure aimed at improving board effectiveness. It is also an accountability tool because the results of the evaluation are disclosed to shareholders who appoint the board.

Various methods are used to assess performance, including self-assessment and external evaluation of board performance. Corporate governance codes do not prescribe the method of assessment but require performance evaluation to be rigorous and transparent. The evaluation should cover performance of individual directors, committees and board leadership. The senior independent director should lead the evaluation of the chairman.

Although board revaluation is now common practice, several boards struggle with the exercise for various reasons, including how to conduct the evaluation, and how to ensure the process is rigorous and leads to improvement. The practice has improved over the years and most countries have governance practitioners and institutions that work with boards on various matters including board evaluation. The key things to note about board evaluation are as follows:

- Boards should periodically evaluate their performance.
- The evaluation exercise should be candid and allow for free expression of views on how the board functions.

- The board should commit time to discussing the results of the evaluation exercise.
- The board should agree on actions for improvement and assign responsibility for the actions.

The company secretary

The requirement to appoint a company secretary

Some organisations are required to appoint a company secretary. In the UK, private companies are exempted from the requirement to appoint a company secretary and anything required to be done by a secretary may be done by a director or person authorised by the directors (section 270 of the Companies Act). However, it is mandatory for public companies to have a company secretary (section 271 of the Companies Act).

Qualifications of the company secretary

The board is responsible for appointing the secretary and is required to ensure that the person has the requisite knowledge and experience to discharge the duties of a secretary. The qualifications of a company secretary are prescribed in section 271(2) of the Companies Act, and it is the responsibility of the board to ensure that the person appointed meets the qualification requirements. These are:

- experience as company secretary for at least three to five years;
- being a member of any of the professional bodies listed in section 271(3);
- being a barrister, advocate or solicitor; and
- being capable of discharging the functions of the secretary.

Although the Companies Act focuses on qualifications of the company secretary, the Cadbury Code made it clear that directors have a duty to appoint a capable person as well as ensure that the person remains capable, and any questions of removal of the secretary are a matter for the board as a whole. The principles of the Cadbury Code have been adopted by other corporate governance standards. For example, the King Code states that:

> ... the governing body should apply its mind to appointing as company secretary or corporate governance professional, a person with the necessary experience, expertise and qualifications, as well

as the appropriate level of seniority to discharge the role effectively
and with the necessary gravitas.

(King IV, p. 91)

The roles of the company secretary

Historically, the role of company secretary was to provide administrative,
compliance and board secretarial functions. However, the role of the
company secretary has been the subject of extensive debate and perhaps
one of the earliest attempts to define the role was in the case of *Panorama
Developments (Guildford) Ltd v Fidelis Furnishing Fabrics Limited
[1971]2QB 711*, where Lord Denning stated:

> Times have changed. A company Secretary is a much more
> important person nowadays than he was in 1887. He is an officer of
> the company with extensive duties and responsibilities. This
> appears not only in the modern Companies Acts but also by the role
> which he plays in the day-to-day business of the companies. He is
> no longer a mere clerk. He regularly makes representations on
> behalf of the company and enters into contracts on its behalf which
> come within the day-to-day running of the company's business…
> He is certainly entitled to sign contracts connected with the admin-
> istrative side of a company's affairs such as employing staff, and
> ordering cars and so forth.

Lord Denning's attempt to expound the role of a company secretary as
stated above is narrow in light of current practice and the responsibilities
of company secretaries. The role has both compliance and governance
responsibilities. The governance responsibilities of the company secretary
were first set out in the Cadbury Code; an extract from the Code is
presented here.

> The company secretary has a key role to play in ensuring that board
> procedures are both followed and regularly reviewed. The chairman
> and the board will look to the company secretary for guidance on
> what their responsibilities are under the rules and regulations to
> which they are subject and on how those responsibilities should be
> discharged. All directors should have access to the advice and
> services of the company secretary and should recognise that the
> chairman is entitled to the strong and positive support of the
> company secretary in ensuring the effective functioning of the

board. It should be standard practice for the company secretary to administer, attend and prepare minutes of board proceedings.

(Cadbury Report, para 4.25)

The above paragraph points to various roles of the company secretary including compliance, advisory, board meetings and board functionality. The King Code states that 'under the direction of the chairman, the company secretary's responsibilities include ensuring good information flows within the board and its committees and between senior management and non-executive directors, as well as facilitating induction and assisting with professional development as required'. In relation to the advisory role, the UK Corporate Governance Code 2018 states that all directors should have access to the advice and services of the company secretary, who is responsible to the board for ensuring that board procedures are complied with. The following are some of the views on the expanded role.

In practice, the role of company secretary has developed into much more than the basic statutory requirements… [compliance, maintaining statutory registers and making filings]. Most notably, the responsibility for developing and implementing processes to promote and sustain good corporate governance has fallen largely within the remit of good corporate governance.

(Deloitte)

No mere servant: The evolving role of the company secretary.

(Blog)

From Housekeeping to Gatekeeping… The role of the Company Secretary has been transformed from that of chief administrator of a company to corporate gatekeeper. This transformation has been driven by the increasing importance of capital markets which require transparency and board independence to ensure investor confidence.

(Joseph Lee)

In light of the above, it is increasingly clear that the company secretary or governance officer is a key governance player, and every board should have an officer responsible for board governance. Some professional bodies, such as the Institute of Chartered Secretaries and Administrators (ICSA), argue that the profile of the company secretary role needs to be raised among other board members.

The executive/management

In any organisation, the board is responsible for oversight, policy formulation and strategic direction among other things. The day-to-day management of the affairs of an organisation is the responsibility of management. The board is responsible for appointing the senior executive/management team, and although the board has overall responsibility for governance, the management is responsible for implementing the policies of the board. It is important for the board to ensure effectiveness of this delegated responsibility.

> The governing body should ensure that the appointment of, and delegation to, competent executive management contributes to an effective arrangement by which authority and responsibilities are exercised.
>
> (King IV)

The executive/senior management are appointed by the board and responsible to the board for overall performance of the organisation. They are key players in the governance of an organisation. First, they provide information that aids decision making at board level. The management has a key role to play in the quality of information that a board receives. This includes receiving it in a timely manner and being able to freely interact and engage with management. The company secretary as a governance officer of the board plays a key role in transmitting information to the board and ensuring that management provides it in a timely manner. Second, it is said that the test of a pudding is in the eating. The test of organisational governance is at management level. This is because although the board has overall responsibility for governance and is required to set the tone at the top, implementation of policies and day-to-day governance are done at management level.

The senior management team is responsible for implementing policies of the board and ensuring that all operations of the organisation are aligned with the governance framework. For example, Chapter 6 discusses ethical leadership and creating an ethical culture within an organisation. The management has an important role to play in creating an ethical culture, particularly in ensuring that an organisation's operations are aligned with the values of the organisation.

Several governance functions are performed by management, including risk governance, compliance governance, IT governance, and

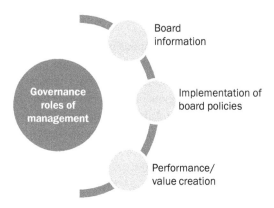

Figure 4.2: The governance roles of management

stakeholder relations. The board has overall responsibility for these, but the actual work is done by the management. The skills and competencies of the management team, relations between board and management, and overall culture within an organisation will all have an impact on how management executes its governance responsibilities. Figure 4.2 illustrates managerial governance roles.

Chapter summary

- The board of directors takes a pre-eminent position in the governance of organisations. However, there are corporate governance players including shareholders, executives and the company secretary. They collectively contribute to the governance of organisations.
- Governance frameworks need to define clearly the roles and responsibilities of the various players as well as ensuring that they are able to function effectively.
- Culture, clarity of roles, reporting, accountability mechanisms are critical to the functioning of the various players.

5   The role of professionals in governance

Introduction

In Chapter 4, the role of the key governance players was discussed. These key players are supported by a number of professionals, the work of which will be explored in this chapter.

The internal audit function

The board is responsible for internal controls and risk management. It should set appropriate policies on internal controls and risk management and seek regular assurances to satisfy itself that the systems it has put in place are functioning effectively.

> UK Corporate Governance Code, 2018
> Audit, Risk and Internal Control
> The board should establish the risk and internal control framework and determine the nature and extent of the principal risks it is willing to take in order to achieve its strategic objectives. The board should satisfy itself that the company's internal controls are robust, and allow for prudent and effective risk assessment and management.

To assist them in ensuring that the internal control and risk management systems are functioning effectively, the board uses internal auditors.

> Internal audit is an independent, objective assurance and consulting activity designed to add value and improve an organization's operations. It helps an organization accomplish its objectives by bringing a systemic, disciplined approach to evaluate and improve the effectiveness of risk management, control and governance processes.
>
> (Chartered Institute of Internal Auditors)

The internal audit function has traditionally been perceived as a monitoring or watchdog function that is not in any way related to the core business of an organisation. However, it is now recognised that it provides a much broader function that includes both assurance and analysis of the operations of an organisation. All this leads to improved governance and the achievement of the organisation's objectives.

Internal audit as part of the third line of assurance remains pivotal to corporate governance. Its role has evolved in recent years for it to contribute insight in the business and furthermore, foresight through the use of pattern recognition, trend assessment, analysis and scenarios. An internal audit function should strive for this level of excellence.

(King IV)

The role and function of internal audit are determined by the governing body. The internal standards for the professional practice of internal auditing provide guidance on the framework for internal audit.

The following should be noted with regard to the internal audit function:

- The internal audit function supports the board to deliver on its mandate of ensuring adequacy of internal controls and risk management.
- The board should have direct oversight of the internal audit function. This is usually delegated to the audit committee, which is responsible for, among other things, the structure and arrangements for the function (in-house or outsourced function, skills and competencies required), appointments, resource allocation, work plans and reports.
- The structure and arrangements for internal audit will vary from one organisation to another. They will depend on the size of the organisation, nature and complexity of operations, and risks among other factors.
- The board, through the audit committee, should ensure independence of the internal audit function by clarifying oversight, supervision and reporting arrangements.
- The internal audit function should be aligned to the overall strategic objectives of the organisation and framework for assessing risks and opportunities for the organisation.
- The governing body/board should annually review the adequacy and effectiveness of internal audit and report on it.

The external audit function

Every company, with the exception in some countries of dormant companies, must have an external auditor. Best practice and the law in most jurisdictions require the external auditor to be independent. To be eligible for appointment as a company's auditor, the person or firm must be a member of a recognised supervisory body. The board is responsible for ensuring that resolutions appointing the external auditor and giving the board the authority to set the remuneration of the auditors are placed before shareholders at the general meeting at which the annual financial statements are laid.

In many jurisdictions, auditors are able to resign as they wish. However, when doing so, they must give notice in writing to the company setting out why they have resigned and any circumstances that should be brought to the attention of the shareholders or creditors. If the auditor discloses circumstances surrounding the resignation, the company should bring these circumstances to the attention of the shareholders and creditors as soon as possible.

The opinion that external auditors give in the annual report and accounts of a company is given to the shareholders. The external auditors' report on compliance with the law and accounting standards and whether the accounts that have been prepared by the board present a true and (in some cases) fair picture of the financial reality of the company. They are not responsible for detecting fraud or errors in the organisation's financial statements. This is the responsibility of the organisation's governing body.

If shareholders are dissatisfied with the auditor, they usually have the power to remove them.

The G20/OECD Principles spell out the key responsibilities of the board. These include ensuring the integrity of accounting and financial reporting systems, including independent audit. In reality it is the management and not the board who handle the relationship with the external auditors. Some countries have tried to make the board, and in some cases even shareholders, more involved in the relationship by giving more responsibility for internal controls and risk management to the non-executive directors and/or shareholders through the audit committee.

The G20/OECD Principles of Corporate Governance

An annual audit should be conducted by an independent, competent and qualified auditor in accordance with high-quality auditing standards. This should ensure that the auditor provides an external and objective assurance to the board and shareholders that the financial statements fairly represent the financial position and performance of the company in all material respects.

In addition to certifying that the financial statements represent fairly the financial position of a company, the audit statement should also include an opinion on the way in which financial statements have been prepared and presented. This should contribute to an improved control environment in the company. In some jurisdictions, the external auditors are also required to report on the company's corporate governance.

The King Code considers external audit as part of the combined assurance mechanism and one line of defence for an organisation that should lead to improved controls, reporting and decision making.

> The governing body should ensure that assurance results in an adequate and effective control environment and integrity of reports for better decision making.
>
> (King IV, Principle 4.5)

The governing body/board should satisfy itself about the integrity of the financial reports of the organisation by ensuring:

- compliance with financial reporting standards. This responsibility is usually delegated to the audit committee and where this is done, the board should satisfy itself that the committee is adequately composed and able to fulfil its mandate. For example, the UK Corporate Governance Code 2018 requires at least one member of the audit committee to have recent and relevant financial experience;
- effective arrangements for oversight over the auditors. The audit committee should have primary responsibility for the appointment and removal of auditors;
- the independence and objectivity of the auditor are assessed periodically;
- significant audit matters and how these were addressed are disclosed; and
- the auditors report to the shareholders and respond to any issues or queries raised in relation to their report. This is usually done at the company's annual general meeting.

Auditor independence

Best practice states that external auditors should be independent from the organisation, so that the audit is not influenced by the relationship between the auditor and the organisation. The organisation should ensure that suitable measures are in place to protect the independence of the auditor. These measures may include the following.

Assessment of independence of audit firm employees

The UK Corporate Governance Code 2018 gives the audit committee the responsibility for reviewing and monitoring the independence and objectivity of the external auditors. The UK FRC Guidance on Audit Committees suggests various measures an audit committee should take in carrying out this role. These include the following:

1. The committee should seek reassurance that the auditors and their staff have no family, financial, employment, investment or business relationship with the organisation that could adversely affect their independence or objectivity.
2. The committee should annually seek information from the audit firm about its policies for maintaining independence and monitoring compliance with relevant requirements.

In practice, most audit firms make presentations to the governing bodies on their independence, without being requested to do so, when they present the annual financial statements.

Non-audit services

To assist in external auditor independence, best practice is growing globally that audit firms that perform an audit for a company (particularly a listed company) should not contemporaneously provide the company with other non-audit services. As we saw in Chapter 3, the EU Audit Regulations have been adopted into law in European Union (EU) countries, including the UK requirements relating to non-audit work.

Examples of some of the prohibited services are:

- management functions;
- human resource functions;
- broker-dealer, investment adviser or investment banking services;
- book-keeping or other services related to accounting records or financial statements;

- design and implementation of financial information systems;
- appraisal or valuation services, fairness opinions or contribution-in-kind reports;
- actuarial services;
- internal audit outsourcing;
- legal services (including company secretarial services);
- expert services; and
- tax services where auditor independence would be impaired.

Best practice, and in some cases a legal requirement (for example, in the EU), requires an organisation to have a policy on the provision of non-audit work by the external auditors. This policy would usually be developed and monitored by the audit committee.

Auditor rotation

Many countries have mandated audit firm rotation, for example, Brazil, Italy and Korea. The mandatory audit firm rotation, which usually requires audit firms to be rotated every seven years, is intended to reduce auditors' incentives to develop long-term relationships with their clients so that their preference for conservative accounting choices may be induced.

In 2014, the EU introduced an Audit Directive and Regulation, requiring 'EU public interest entities' to change their audit firm at least every ten years. This rule came into force from 2016. There is an option, however, that mandatory rotation is necessary only every 20 years so long as the rules for annual tendering of the audit every ten years are complied with.

Whether audit firm rotation should be made mandatory is an issue that has been debated for almost five decades in the USA and around the world. Proponents of mandatory audit firm rotation have argued that a new auditor would bring to bear greater scepticism and a fresh perspective that may be lacking in long-standing auditor-client relationships. They have also claimed that when a company has been a client of an audit firm for a number of years, the client can be viewed as a source of a perpetual annuity, potentially impairing the auditor's independence. Conversely, opponents of mandatory firm rotation have argued that audit quality would suffer under such a regime because the auditor would lack familiarity with the client and its industry. Furthermore, opponents have pointed to a higher incidence of problem audits in the early years of the auditor-client relationship than in the later years.

The Institute of Chartered Accountants in Australia responded in December 2011 to the US Public Company Accounting Oversight Board proposals to introduce mandatory audit rotation. The Institute outlined the following to the arguments against mandatory rotation:

- decreased audit quality due to the knowledge lost when the audit firm changes;
- increased audit costs due to high learning curve each incoming audit firm faces;
- increased client costs associated with the incoming audit firm becoming familiar with the business;
- difficulty for the audit committee in choosing a new audit firm that has the relevant industry experience and expertise; and
- difficulty for the audit committee in choosing firms for its non-audit services.

In countries where audit firm rotation is not mandatory, best practice requires leading partners to rotate off the client after five years and be subject to a five-year 'time out' period. Other audit partners should rotate every seven years and have two-year 'time out' periods. This, it is argued, prevents audit firms from getting too comfortable with the company, but still leads to continuity of knowledge.

It should be noted that current regulations in most countries favour audit partner rotation rather than audit firm rotation.

Lawyers

The role of the corporate lawyer is to provide primarily management with legal advice on many aspects of the organisation's business including contract law, tax law, accounting, securities law, bankruptcy, intellectual property rights and licensing, and to carry out due diligence for company transactions. In addition, corporate lawyers may also be asked to advise the board on the legality of certain transactions the organisation is considering, for example, a merger, acquisition or disposal, or where a company seeks an Initial Public Offering (IPO).

The challenge, as we saw in Chapter 1, is that the legal advice given is often based on laws and regulations that set minimum standards. This may create conflicts of interest if the in-house lawyer is also carrying out the governance role in the organisation, which is common in many jurisdictions. This is because in giving both the legal and the governance advice during the board meeting, the lawyer is asked to 'take sides' – that is, in providing legal advice to take the minimum standard route, which may from the management's perspective be the most cost-effective route, rather than what may be seen as a costlier long-term approach that a governance professional may take. This dilemma may compromise the independence and impartiality of the person being asked to provide the advice, both of which are critical to someone carrying out the governance role. If the legal and governance roles are split, both options can be placed before the board with equal emphasis. It is then the board's decision which way the organisation goes. This does not mean that a qualified lawyer cannot act in-house as the organisation's governance officer, only that in doing so, they should seek to avoid such conflicts. For instance, they should not carry out any legal work for the organisation.

Compliance officers

The role of a compliance officer is to provide assurance that an organisation is conducting its business in full compliance with all national and international laws and regulations that pertain to its particular industry, as well as professional standards, accepted business practices and internal standards.

Compliance officers also have a role in educating those who work within a particular organisation and instituting practices that ensure the highest level of compliance. They need to be aware of the organisation's culture and ensure that it is ethical and focused on maintaining the highest level of compliance.

Compliance officers are most often found in health care and banking, and are an important part of the corporate governance framework of an organisation. They give assurance to the board that the organisation is managed in compliance with all relevant laws, regulations, standards and codes.

The International Compliance Association breaks down the role of a compliance officer into two levels of responsibility:

- Level 1: compliance with the external rules that are imposed upon an organisation as a whole; and
- Level 2: compliance with internal systems of control that are imposed to achieve compliance with the externally imposed rules.

The role of professional and other bodies in governance

There are many professional and other bodies around the globe that regulate and set standards of conduct for their professions or members, provide training and guidance for their members and the wider community, and develop best practices in corporate governance. The main ones are listed below.

The Institute of Chartered Secretaries and Administrators (ICSA)

The ICSA is the worldwide qualifying body for chartered secretaries and governance professionals. The organisation qualifies people who have roles as company secretaries, governance advisers, risk managers, compliance managers, etc.

The ICSA, at the time of writing, consists of nine divisions worldwide (Australia, Canada, Hong Kong/China, Malaysia, New Zealand, Singapore, Southern Africa, UKRIAT [UK, Republic of Ireland & Associated Territories] and Zimbabwe), and has approximately 30,000 members in 80 countries.

The ICSA supports its members through expert advice and training, and the provision of resources and guidance, and qualifies students through its international qualifying scheme. It also brings its influence to bear on international trade bodies, governments, regulators, NGOs and companies to represent the views and current thinking of those involved in governance.

The ICSA has a professional standards committee whose role is to maintain standards across the profession. In addition, each of its divisions operates codes of conduct for their members, graduates and students.

Website: www.icsaglobal.org

The Corporate Secretaries International Association (CSIA)

The CSIA is an international federation of professional bodies that promotes the best practices in corporate secretarial, corporate governance and compliance services. It is the international federation of governance professional bodies for corporate secretaries and governance professionals, and represents those who work as frontline practitioners of governance throughout the world. It is recognised by the OECD as the global voice of for this industry and its representatives sit on the OECD corporate governance roundtables.

The CSIA was established in 2010 as a not-for-profit organisation committed to improving the recognition and understanding of the practice of corporate secretaryship and the role of the corporate secretary, and to work to improve governance standards in general.

The CSIA is a global organisation with 16 national organisation members representing some 70,000 corporate secretaries in more than 70 countries (at the time of writing). Its ranks are collectively responsible for delivering four roles: compliance, advice, support and professional administration (made up from legal, governance, ethics, business finance, accounting, secretarial, strategic and administration professionals).

Website: www.csiaorg.com

The Association of Chartered Certified Accountants (ACCA)

The ACCA is the global body for professional accountants. Its expertise and opinion is sought worldwide by governments, professional bodies, academic institutions, employers and the media. It offers a global professional accountancy qualification. At the time of writing, the ACCA has 188,000 fully qualified members and 480,000 students worldwide.

The ACCA provides guidance and advice on governance and risk. For example, in December 2015, it published a series of four reports aimed at assisting boards in their understanding of the impact of corporate culture on behaviour in their organisations.

Website: www.accaglobal.com

In addition to the ACCA, many countries have their own local accounting bodies which offer local qualifications and enforce codes of conduct on their members.

The International Federation of Accountants (IFAC)

The IFAC is the global body for the accountancy profession responsible for strengthening the global accountancy profession by:
- supporting the development of high-quality international standards;
- promoting the adoption and implementation of these standards;
- building the capacity of professional accountancy organisations; and
- speaking out on public interest issues.

At the time of writing, IFAC comprises over 175 members and associates in more than 130 countries and jurisdictions. This represents almost 3 million accountants in public practice, education, government service, industry and commerce.

Law societies

In many countries, law societies also play a part in providing governance and compliance advice to their members. They also operate qualifying schemes and ensure professional standards for their members.

The Institute of Internal Auditors (IIA)

The IIA is the international professional body for internal auditors. Its members work in internal auditing, risk management, governance, internal control, information technology audit, education and security. At the time of writing, the IIA comprises 160 chapters serving 70,000 members globally. IIA provides, among other things, global professional networking, advocacy, training, certification, standards and guidance, research, executive development and career opportunities.

The Institute of Risk Management (IRM)

The IRM is the leading body for professional risk management. It provides globally recognised qualifications and training, publishes research and guidance, and sets professional standards for its members. At the time of writing, the IRM has 6,000 members across all industries in the public, private and not-for-profit sectors.

Many countries have set up local risk management institutes, for example, in Canada and South Africa.

Corporate governance institutes

Corporate governance institutes are being set up in many countries around the world. They provide a variety of services to their members and other stakeholder groups including networking, training, advocacy and corporate governance code development. For example, the Caribbean Corporate Governance Institute has developed the Trinidad and Tobago Code of Corporate Governance for listed companies. Hawkamah, the Institute of Corporate Governance in Dubai, and the Institute of Corporate Governance Uganda have also developed corporate governance codes for SMEs.

Institutes of directors (IODs)

Institutes of directors are also being set up in many countries. These institutes, like the corporate governance institutes, provide a variety of services to their members and other stakeholder groups including networking, training, advocacy and corporate governance code development. For example, the Institute of Directors of Southern Africa was instrumental in the development of the King Codes of Corporate Governance.

Several IODs, such as in the UK and Southern Africa, also promote directorship as a profession. A professional qualification scheme to become a chartered director is offered. Once qualified, a director is expected to comply with a code of conduct and partake in continuing professional development.

Chapter summary

- Many professionals are represented within the governance framework of organisations.
- It is important that their roles are recognised and that these professionals work together to ensure the governance framework works effectively.

6 Stakeholder engagement

Introduction

This chapter explains the rationale and value of stakeholder engagement. There is a growing awareness within organisations that it is important for their success that the interests of stakeholders are taken into consideration when making decisions.

Definition of stakeholders

The International Integrated Reporting Council (IIRC) defines stakeholders as 'Those groups or individuals that can reasonably be expected to be significantly affected by an organisation's business activities, outputs or outcomes, or whose actions can reasonably be expected to significantly affect the ability of the organisation to create value over time'. King IV, the South African Corporate Governance Code, differentiates between external and internal stakeholders, defining them as follows:

- External stakeholders may be material or immaterial to the organisation, external to the organisation and could include customers, consumers, suppliers, trade unions, civil society organisations and government.
- Internal stakeholders are always material stakeholders, are 'directly affiliated with the organisation and include its governing body, management, employees and shareholders'.

A stakeholder is, therefore, someone who has an interest in or expectation of something from an organisation. Stakeholders are usually affected by what the organisation does or does not do. They may also, if they are a key stakeholder, have influence or power over the organisation and so may be able to influence how an organisation behaves and the decisions it takes. For this reason, many argue that managing differing stakeholder interests and the influence/power that stakeholders have over an organisation should be part of any corporate governance debate.

Approaches to corporate governance: attitude to stakeholders

As we saw in Chapter 1, the different approaches to corporate governance treat stakeholders differently.

- The stakeholder approach argues that organisations should aim to have regard to all stakeholder views, not just those of shareholders, when making decisions.
- The stakeholder inclusive approach argues that the organisation should take into account the legitimate and reasonable needs, interests and expectations of all material stakeholders when making decisions in the best long-term interests of the organisation. King IV states that this approach allows organisations 'to give parity to all sources of value creation' including human, intellectual, social and environmental capital, not just financial capital.
- The enlightened shareholder approach argues that when making decisions, organisations should look to shareholder value in the long term, not just the short term, and in doing so they will therefore have to take into consideration some stakeholder interests in addition to the interests of shareholders.
- The shareholder value approach argues that an organisation's purpose is to maximise shareholder value. Milton Friedman stated that 'few trends could so thoroughly undermine the foundations of our free society as the acceptance by corporate officials of a social responsibility other than to make as much money for their stock-holders as possible'. In this approach it is up to the shareholders to define the business of the organisation. Directors are accountable only to shareholders for their decisions, not to a wider stakeholder group.

Most organisations' first priority under the laws and regulations that set them up is to act in the best interests of the organisation. Some, as we have seen above, believe this to be at odds with meeting stakeholders' needs. Many more are starting to see that organisations cannot ignore stakeholder expectations when conducting their strategic thinking and decision making. They need to identify as part of their strategic planning and decision making processes the level of interest of key stakeholders and the power those stakeholders have in impressing their expectations on the organisation's strategic choices.

However, the challenge for organisations when including any stakeholder interests in their decision-making or strategic planning processes is that different stakeholders have different interests, and these interests may be in conflict. Organisations have to decide and communicate who their key stakeholders are and which of their needs, interests and expectations they are going to be taking into account when developing the organisation's culture, structure and strategy. Evidence suggests that this is the only way that organisations can have a sustainable business in the long term.

Business case for stakeholder engagement

Evidence shows that organisations that successfully engage with their stakeholders are also successful in their business. The benefits of effective stakeholder engagement for organisations are as follows:

- Build and strengthen a good reputation and brand recognition.
- Create value and wealth.
- Gain and retain loyal customers while avoiding boycotts or other undesirable consumer actions.
- Be perceived as a more desirable place to work and have an easier time recruiting and retaining talented staff members.
- Identify ways to increase efficiency and reduce costs in their operations.
- Have a more responsible approach to risk-taking which reduces risk.
- Be better able to leverage opportunities, giving them competitive advantage as they are able to identify new ideas for products or services that address stakeholder needs. Effective stakeholder engagement promotes corporate learning and innovation.
- Can be more readily welcomed into new markets, as existing organisations embedded in those markets perceive them as less hostile to local values and ways of operating.

Organisations that do not engage their stakeholders risk becoming very management-centric, which can lead to a limited perspective of the organisation, its capabilities and its potential. One advantage of non-executive directors is that they can bring an external perspective to management. If an organisation does not have appropriately skilled non-executive directors, it becomes more important for the organisation to engage with stakeholders to get this external perspective.

Stakeholder method for measuring organisational wealth

One method of measuring organisational wealth is the stakeholder method. This combines the value of both the organisation's tangible and intangible assets with the value of relational assets, such as stakeholder relationships and reputation. Other measures focus on resources or the organisation's position in the industry. It is believed that organisations that view wealth creation as a function of resources or market position are less likely to share information and be collaborative, creating barriers as a means to preserve wealth rather than linkages and collaborations.

Post *et al.* (2002) identified how different stakeholders contributed to an organisation's wealth. Obviously the value from this contribution only materialises if an organisation engages with the stakeholder to maximise the benefit of the relationship. Table 6.1 is adapted from their findings.

Table 6.1: Stakeholder contributions to an organisation's wealth

Stakeholder	Contribution to wealth
Investors	• Capital through equity or debt • Financial market recognition that could lead to reduced risk and borrowing costs
Employees/ unions	• Provision and development of human capital • Productive and collaborative workplace • Workforce stability • Conflict resolution
Suppliers	• Network and supply chain efficiencies • Collaborative, cost reducing processes and technologies
Customers	• Brand and reputation • Repeated and related purchasers • Collaborative design, development and problem solving
Creditors	• Reduced borrowing costs • Lower collateral requirement • Relational partnership
Communities	• Trust • License to operate • Mutual support and accommodation of operational practices

Stakeholder	Contribution to wealth
Governments	• Macroeconomic and social policies that favour the organisation • No/lesser political interference
Regulators	• Validation of operations including quality and reliability of products or services

Effective stakeholder engagement can be used as a mechanism for reducing an organisation's risks – reputational, financial, etc. This is particularly true for companies with strong brand recognition. Unilever, as can be seen from the following case study, changed its policy on advertising brands in response to stakeholder requests.

CASE STUDY: UNILEVER

Unilever up until the mid-2000s had a policy of only advertising its brands, not Unilever the organisation. This was to protect brands from cross-contamination should there be a problem with one of the company's major brands. If you asked people in the street to name a Unilever brand, they might well have struggled, although the brands were found in all homes. The change in Unilever's policy was caused by a demand to know what Unilever's products were. At the time, Unilever the organisation was receiving great acclaim for its sustainability and corporate responsibility policies (see Chapter 5 for examples). The public wanted to reward Unilever's actions by buying its brands rather than those of its competitors, which were seen as being not as proactive in this area. Unilever took a decision in the mid-2000s that was seen as being in the best interests of the organisation to sell itself as the brand. Unilever's products are therefore now sold under the Unilever brand.

Stakeholders and innovation

Engaging with stakeholders can also bring innovation in an organisation. For example:

Professor Muhammad Yunus' interactions with the poor in Bangladesh led to the invention of the first microfinance organisation, Grameen Bank.

In 2002, Hindustani Lever commenced a five-year project in India to encourage school children to hand-wash and bathe with soap. The project was known as Lifebuoy Swasthya Chetna ('Health Awakening'). By 2007, 80 million people in 27,000 villages had been involved in the project. The project led Unilever to develop a small affordable bar of soap weighing 18 grams which provided a person with 10 weeks of once-a-day hand and face washing.

The founder of outdoor clothing brand Patagonia, Yvon Chouinard, was asked to talk at a sustainable fisheries conference. Following his talk, he left frustrated by the ignorance of his audience. 'They didn't know what they were doing,' he said of the seafood merchants. 'They had no idea about toxins, about incidental catch. Their customers are all going to want to know this stuff soon. Restaurants will want to know' (WSJ.com April 2012). Despite having zero knowledge of the food business, Chouinard launched his own salmon fishery, Patagonia Provisions, in April 2012, to show the fishing industry how it could be done.

Adopting stakeholder engagement

The ICSA/Core Partnership Poll, published in April 2017, found that 73% of the organisations polled actively considered the view of their wider stakeholder base when taking decisions. Only 11% of respondents felt that their boards did not. Organisations captured stakeholder views through (among other things) employee and customer surveys, feedback, test environments, focus groups, roadshows and regular meetings with key investors.

Stakeholder engagement allows organisations to detect, assess and manage changes in their societal environment that may prove critical for their reputation and hence the ability to implement their strategy, create value and remain sustainable in the long term. An organisation does not exist as an island; it is an integral part of society. Therefore, boards of organisations should be aware of society's expectations of and interests in their organisations. This means that:

- stakeholder engagement should be integrated into the core functions of the board, policy setting, accountability and control, and the selection of executive management; and
- management and staff should be empowered and instructed to engage positively with the organisation's stakeholders.

Once organisations have adopted a policy of stakeholder engagement, they should carry out the following tasks:

- Identify who their stakeholders are that have legitimate expectations and interests.
- Map the power and interest of the particular stakeholder or stakeholder group so that they can develop a strategy for engaging with them.
- Identify, discuss and prioritise the key risks associated with changing societal expectations.
- Determine the board's financial and non-financial needs for decision making, management oversight, and monitoring key stakeholder relationships associated with creating value and long-term sustainability.
- Discuss and approve key performance indicators for social, environmental and financial performance.
- Approve a policy for external reporting, and financial, non-financial (sustainability) or integrated reporting.
- Look to integrate stakeholder issues into annual shareholder meetings. This can be done through the presentations made at the meeting and/or displays at the entrance or in the hall.
- Discuss the risks and impacts (positive and negative) of projects and operations and provide transparent disclosure information to stakeholders (including shareholders).
- Convene stakeholder forums and invite key stakeholder representatives to address board meetings so that members of boards hear directly what the stakeholders' concerns and issues are.
- Document the concerns and issues of stakeholders and lessons learned and feed this into the risk management, strategic planning and business continuity processes so that the organisation is able to leverage opportunities and lessen the negative impact.
- Recognise that different stakeholder groups may have different interests and ideas. Tailor engagement and dialogue to help the board better represent these disparate interests and also to help the stakeholders understand why the board has made a particular decision.
- Develop policies on who within the organisation should be the prime communicator for which stakeholder group.

Once an organisation identifies who its stakeholders are, it can make informed decisions about balancing the interests of all groups to which the organisation has some obligation. Organisations should then communicate on what basis decisions have been made, so stakeholders understand how and why a particular decision has been made. By doing this organisations will build and improve relationships with their stakeholders, which in turn should make it easier for the organisation to operate, create value and be sustainable in the long term.

Identifying stakeholders and their roles

Stakeholders can take many different roles, including the following.

Customers

Organisations can carry out focus groups or surveys to get input from customers on particular products or services. This information can then be analysed and fed into research and development (R&D), strategic planning, etc.

Suppliers

Information from suppliers, for example on demand for supplies, availability of supplies, costs, different sources of materials, etc., can be very useful to the board in its decision making. Other stakeholder groups also expect organisations to apply the same values to their supply chains, so engagement with suppliers can reassure organisations that there will be no surprises from their supply chain. Many organisations have been caught out in the past – for example, Nike and child labour, or the Body Shop and testing on animals.

Creditors

Through engagement with their creditors, organisations can find out about alternative sources of finance, negotiate better credit terms, etc.

Regulators

Engagement with regulators allows organisations to understand better how regulations apply to them. Where there are difficulties in applying certain regulations, organisations can lobby the government for changes.

Representatives of special interest groups

These representatives come from local communities, environmental groups, etc. Organisations can invite these stakeholders to participate in focus groups or on panels to give their views on the organisation's practices or potential new projects.

Co-implementers

Co-implementers include NGOs, governments, etc. who have partnered with an organisation to implement a joint solution or programme to address a shared challenge, such as Unilever and health issues – Blueband, Lifebuoy Soap.

Experts

Consultants, technical advisers, academics, etc. may be invited by the organisation to contribute knowledge or strategic advice to the organisation's board. An organisation may also set up an advisory panel to give advice on scientific or ethical issues, and invite this group to sit on the panel due to their expertise.

Co-monitors

Organisations may enter into agreements with local communities or interest groups whereby both the stakeholder and the organisation co-monitor the outcome of an organisation supported project – for example, cleaning up a river.

Media

Organisations can help build their reputation by engaging with the media. They would also hope that by building a relationship with journalists, the latter would give them the benefit of the doubt and check with them on a story that could damage the organisation's reputation.

Reasons for stakeholder interests

Organisations in developing stakeholder strategies have to engage with different stakeholder groups to be able to understand their expectations and the extent to which they are likely to show an active interest in the strategy and decision making of the organisation or seek to influence it (see Table 6.2).

Table 6.2: Reasons for stakeholder interest

Stakeholder	Reason for interest
Investor, shareholder	Potential or actual stake in the company
Employees	Continuity of employment, ability to pay salaries and benefits
Suppliers	Continuity of demand of product or service
Customers	Continuity of supply of product or service
Financial institutions such as pension funds, insurance companies, etc.	Financial stake in the organisation
Creditors	Interested in future cash flows, the security if debts
Media	Newsworthy stories they can present to their audiences
Government, regulators	Ensure no abuse of public interest
Civil society, NGO pressure groups, etc.	Ensure responsible corporate behaviour
The public	Variable interests

Organisations should think out of the box when identifying the stakeholders with whom they should be engaging. Many saw the Coca-Cola Company's partnership with the World Wildlife Fund as strange when it was announced in 2007, since they had been adversaries in the past. However, the partnership, which is aimed at conserving the world's freshwater resources, is still ongoing ten years later.

Stakeholder mapping

Once an organisation has identified its key stakeholders, it should decide what kind of relationship to develop with that particular stakeholder. To do this, organisations have to analyse and then map their stakeholders' interests and the power they have. Figure 6.1 shows how once an organisation has identified the power a particular stakeholder has over it or the level of interest a particular stakeholder has in it, a relationship could be adopted for that particular stakeholder.

The questions an organisation should be asking when carrying out a mapping exercise are as follows:

- Who are the stakeholders the organisation has to engage with?
- What does the organisation think the stakeholders' needs, interests or expectations are?
- What responsibilities and obligations does the organisation have to the different stakeholders?
- Where are these stakeholders currently on the matrix?
- Should any of the stakeholders be in a different quadrant?
- Are there too many stakeholders in a single quadrant?
- If so, what strategies could the organisation develop to move the position of any of the stakeholders?
- Does the stakeholder engagement create any opportunities or challenges for the organisation?
- If so, what strategies could the organisation develop to take advantage of the opportunities or solve/lessen the impact of the challenges?

The answers to these questions can help an organisation to develop strategies for stakeholder engagement.

The four quadrants in Figure 6.1 suggest different relationship types with a stakeholder:

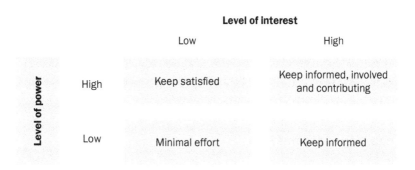

Figure 6.1: Stakeholder matrix

1. Stakeholders who have high power and high interest are an organisation's 'key' stakeholders. These are the stakeholders that the board should focus on and ensure wherever possible that their needs, interests and expectations are met. There should be an ongoing relationship and engagement with them to ensure they are receiving all the information they need to keep contributing to the organisation. An example of this group is employees.

2. Stakeholders who have high interest but low levels of power will need to be kept informed of what is happening in the organisation. From time to time these stakeholders may need to be given more power to secure their buy-in to a proposed strategic change. An example of this group is small retail shareholders.

3. Stakeholders who have high power but low interest can potentially be the most dangerous for an organisation. An example is a provider of financial capital. They may decide to withdraw their support at any time. Organisations will need to try to keep this group satisfied with any requirement they may have. They may also want to try to increase the level of interest this group may have – for example, through developing a stronger relationship, e.g. relationship banking.

4. Stakeholders who have low interest and low power do not typically require much attention. Often the general public fall into this category. As has been seen in several recent cases, e.g. Starbucks and Google, where the public has to varying degrees boycotted the services of both over tax planning strategies, they cannot be totally forgotten about.

Organisations will need to monitor and consider the stakeholders in all four quadrants in their decision making and strategic planning processes, to ensure that they do not move position and create reputational risk for the organisation. Organisations may also have to develop mechanisms for involving stakeholders in their decisions, such as through customer surveys and focus groups. As mentioned above, strategies for influencing stakeholders may also have to be developed, especially if the organisation is wanting the stakeholder to move quadrant.

Engaging stakeholders

'No surprises' is one of the most important principles of good corporate governance. Frequently reputable organisations are finding themselves caught in what appears to them to be a surprise controversy, despite professional public relations work and elaborate mechanisms of internal control. Business leaders are starting to recognise that their traditional approaches to running their organisations are insufficient to handle changing societal expectations around the globe. They are starting to realise that stakeholder engagement is important to business success and societal trust.

There is no one strategy for engaging with stakeholders. Each organisation has to work out its own based on the stakeholders it has identified and the impact the organisation's operations have. Organisations will also have to recognise that an issue that is a priority for them may not always be a priority for a stakeholder, and so the stakeholder may not want to engage or enter into a partnership at that time. A long-term patient approach by an organisation may therefore be necessary.

Prior to commencing any stakeholder engagement, an organisation must ensure that it meets its economic and legal responsibilities, through creating value for its investors and complying with government laws and regulations. Stakeholder interests can sometimes conflict with these interests, especially in the short term. Organisations may have to take the long-term view, and as part of their business continuity planning work towards changing legal requirements or stakeholder views.

When considering the long-term implications of responding to an immediate stakeholder concern, organisations may choose not to engage with that particular stakeholder in the interests of a larger stakeholder group. For example, mining organisations have found that investing in the immediate community can create jealousy among neighbouring communities.

If an organisation chooses to engage with its shareholders, it can do so in one of three ways:

1. Reactively – the organisation engages defensively when forced to in response to a crisis, usually in an attempt to rebuild an organisation's reputation.

2. Proactively – the organisation tries to understand its stakeholders' concerns and issues:
   - The organisation can do this through research or eliciting views from particular stakeholder groups and then take into account in its decision-making process what it understands are stakeholder interests. Organisations carry out customer surveys, focus

groups, shareholder surveys, competitor research, etc. This information then feeds into the decision-making process.

- The organisation can engage directly with stakeholders to get their input on what decisions should be made and then makes the decision itself. This is often the case with shareholders and their representative bodies. Organisations will run a proposal or idea past some larger shareholders to get their views before making a final decision on a particular issue, such as remuneration packages for directors or senior executives.
- The organisation involves stakeholders in the decision-making process. An organisation could get stakeholders together – employees, the community, etc. – and ask them to vote on a particular action. For example, LaFarge Cement involved the community members in Morocco in the process of finding a new location for a cement plant.

3. Interactively – the organisation has ongoing relationships of mutual respect, openness and trust with stakeholders. The organisation can do this through many of the channels mentioned in point 2.

An example of where a company engaged with stakeholders effectively, as part of the crisis management of an event, is Pick 'n Pay Supermarkets, whose products were poisoned with cyanide (see case study below). In this case, the company engaged its customers as soon as it was found that their safety was in jeopardy. Rather than the incident being detrimental to the company's performance and reputation, it actually had the opposite effect. The share price rose and Pick 'n Pay, in a national survey, was subsequently rated the most trusted company in South Africa.

CASE STUDY: PICK 'N PAY – SOUTH AFRICAN SUPERMARKET

In May 2003, an anonymous caller phoned Pick 'n Pay to say that he had sent by insured post a parcel containing four products that had been poisoned with cyanide. The caller claimed that unless ransom instructions were followed, similar items would be placed randomly in stores. Tests confirmed that the products sent contained traces of cyanide. The extortionist stated to the CEO that customers would not be harmed if instructions were followed. A 'dialogue' on how to deliver the ransom began, but the ransom was never collected.

Less than a month later, the extortionist made a call to tell the company that he had randomly placed four items in a store, each marked 'Poisoned, do not consume. Contact Pick 'n Pay immediately'. An immediate search was mounted and three marked items were found. Arrangements were made to withdraw all units of these lines, regardless of whether they showed signs of tampering. Soon after, a woman called Pick 'n Pay's call centre to say she had become very ill when she consumed a can of sardines. On looking at the packaging she saw it had been marked 'Poisoned, do not consume. Contact Pick 'n Pay immediately.'

After this incident, Pick 'n Pay decided to bring the situation to the attention of the public. As the CEO stated, 'The second customer safety was placed in jeopardy, it was time for everyone to know.' As soon as the company went public, it faced a barrage of calls from customers claiming they had become ill after eating products from Pick 'n Pay. The retailer immediately recalled from the shelves any of the products that had been identified as suspect. In addition, Pick 'n Pay said it was prepared to reimburse the medical expenses regardless of whether the incident was a proven poison case or an incorrectly diagnosed stomach upset.

Pick 'n Pay feared that its future custom was seriously threatened. The company estimated a loss of R15 million through expensive advertising, product withdrawal and specialist consultants.

Two weeks later, the CEO reported that he had heard nothing from the extortionist but that the company would maintain high security. He promised the public that as soon as the company heard from the extortionist, 'You will know about it.'

In the two-day period after Pick 'n Pay went public, it received over 1,000 supportive calls. Its customers frequented the store as usual. People expressed their appreciation for the honest and direct way in which Pick 'n Pay was handling the crisis. Another sign of support was the share performance. Shares were trading at R13.60 late on the Monday after Pick 'n Pay went public with the matter. These shares were up on Friday's closing price of R13.56, despite a short-lived dip to R13. Clearly, investors felt part of the Pick 'n Pay supportive community too.

At the end of 2003, in a national survey, Pick 'n Pay was rated the most trusted company in South Africa. The company's high rating was attributed to its excellent communication with stakeholders, the perception that it practised what it preached and a widely held belief that it cared about its reputation.

(Taken from International Finance Corporation: Corporate Secretaries ToolKit)

Some engagements have fixed timetables to ensure that results are achieved. The timetable should be developed based on input from all parties. It is important to establish ground rules for public disclosure and managing expenses related to the engagement. Organisations should avoid giving money to stakeholder groups as part of the engagement, as this could be misconstrued as a bribe. Any money that is paid over should be documented, giving the reason for it, and reported.

Organisations should not forget to communicate internally to employees the purpose of the engagement and what the organisation seeks to achieve from it, so that a consistent message is communicated from the organisation.

Where issues and concerns which are raised as part of a stakeholder engagement cannot be addressed, an organisation should be honest and transparent about why this is the case. For example, many pharmaceutical organisations are asked by stakeholders to eliminate their use of animal testing, but many governments require animal tests for product approval. Novo Nordisk, the world's largest maker of insulin products for diabetics, acknowledges that reducing its reliance on animal testing is desirable, but it can only do so if and when governments are convinced to change the approvals process. The organisation publicly reports on the number of animals used in testing and the organisation's success in changing or influencing government policies on product testing.

Not all corporate disclosures are helpful. It is important for organisations to ensure that all their communications are timely, accurate and reliable, comprehensive, balanced and relevant to the stakeholder group. Where necessary comparable information to competitors, previous targets should be provided to assist the stakeholder in making their judgements about the organisation's performance or decision making.

Browne and Nuttall (2013) set out some of the most common reasons and some suggestions as to how organisations could do better. Table 6.3 is based on their findings.

Table 6.3: External engagement with stakeholders

Question	Reasons
Why are organisations failing to build stronger relations with external stakeholders?	Reasons for failure include: • struggles to meet high expectations of citizens and governments that organisations will solve economic, environmental and social problems; • increased levels of scrutiny; • a focus on protecting the organisation's reputation – in order to get away with irresponsible behaviour elsewhere; • short-lived CSR programmes disconnected from the organisation's strategy; • over-reliance on a centralised CSR team at the head office, operating without full support of the business and without an understanding of local stakeholders and local contexts; • high-profile but relatively cheap propaganda initiatives; and • glossy annual reviews of little progress.
How can organisations do better?	Organisations that succeed in building profitable relationships with the external world: • develop integrated engagement strategies to gain stakeholder trust before a crisis hits; • define themselves through what they contribute to society – capital, jobs, skills ideas and taxes; • have a strategy and vision similar to that of Unilever: 'To double the company's sales while reducing its environmental impact'; • have leadership that puts the organisation's reputation on the line and get buy-in from people in the organisation; • know their individual and institutional stakeholders as well as they know their customers; • are prepared to invest in learning about stakeholders at their corporate and local market level; and • see their understanding of stakeholders as an advantage over the competition.

Question	Reasons
How can organisations do better?	• build senior management teams who value integrated external engagement through on-the-job experience and training in such areas as negotiation; • help employees value integrated external engagement; • incorporate integrated external engagement into the business processes such as setting corporate strategy, designing products and planning projects; • measure outcomes and reward successful results in engaging with stakeholders; and • recognise that the aim is not to please everyone. Sometimes a mutually advantageous solution is impossible.

The ICSA/Core Partnership Poll published in April 2017 found that some respondents felt they could do better at their stakeholder engagement. When questioned about what they could do to improve their stakeholder engagement, the responses included:

- more openness and transparency;
- increased use of social media;
- directors spending more time with the business and speaking with stakeholders in the communities that the business works in;
- continually reviewing their stakeholder base and working out how to engage with individual stakeholder groups;
- evolving their strategies regarding stakeholders;
- allowing sufficient time to receive and consider stakeholder views before decisions needed to be made; and
- putting employees higher up the list of priorities. It was felt that if employees were on the organisation's side, it would help with other stakeholder engagement.

The Global Corporate Governance Forum and the International Finance Corporation in their publication 'Stakeholder Engagement and the Board: Integrating Best Governance Practices' set out guidelines for organisations when developing strategies for engaging with stakeholders. Table 6.4 summarises these guidelines.

Table 6.4: Best practices for engaging with stakeholders

Guidance	Description
Start early.	Relationships take time to build. The organisation and the stakeholder need to build mutual trust and respect. It is difficult to do this in times of crisis. Engagement should therefore be started early and developed so that when a crisis comes, the relationship is in place.
Keep an open mind.	Organisations should enter discussions with stakeholders with an open mind. This is because the outcome of stakeholder engagements cannot be predetermined. Attempts by organisations to dominate discussions may be perceived with suspicion by a stakeholder who may come to see the approach as a public relations exercise, and not a true wish to engage to the benefit of both parties.
Tailor engagement practices.	Engagement practices should be tailored to the needs of both the organisation and the stakeholder. As we saw in Chapter 5, partnerships where there is a 'win-win' relationship are likely to be sustainable and give benefits to both parties. Organisations should explain the purpose of the partnership, and agree with the stakeholder what information and actions will be required by both parties. The information on the partnership to be disclosed and by whom should also be agreed.
Management engagement as part of the business model of the organisation.	Stakeholder engagement should be seen by the business as being part of the organisation's strategy and business operations. By doing this, the partnership is more likely to be sustainable and create value for both the organisation and the stakeholder. If both the organisation and the stakeholder can see the benefit the partnership evidence shows they are more likely to try to maintain it even when times get tough. Clear and direct reporting lines and the involvement of senior management, at both the organisation and stakeholder, are also important for the success of a partnership. The arrangement should be treated like any business arrangement.

Guidance	Description
Take the long-term view.	If the cause of the engagement is an intrinsic part of the organisation's business model and hence related to the organisation's strategy, then organisations should try to develop a long-term, ongoing dialogue with the stakeholder, rather than ad hoc or one-off discussions.

In September 2017, ICSA: The Governance Institute collaborated with the Investment Association to publish the following ten core principles for boards engaging with stakeholders:

1. Boards should identify, and keep under regular review, who they consider their key stakeholders to be and why.
2. Boards should determine which stakeholders they need to engage with directly, as opposed to relying solely on information from management.
3. When evaluating their composition and effectiveness, boards should identify what stakeholder expertise is needed in the board room and decide whether they have, or would benefit from, directors with directly relevant experience or understanding.
4. When recruiting any director, the nomination committee should take the stakeholder perspective into account when deciding on the recruitment process and the selection criteria.
5. The chairman (supported by the company secretary) should keep under review the adequacy of the training received by all directors on stakeholder-related matters, and the induction received by new directors, particularly those without previous board experience.
6. The chairman (supported by the board, management and the company secretary) should determine how best to ensure that the board's decision-making processes give sufficient consideration to key stakeholders.
7. Boards should ensure that appropriate engagement with key stakeholders is taking place and that this is kept under regular review.
8. In designing engagement mechanisms, companies should consider what would be most effective and convenient for the stakeholders, not just the company.
9. The board should report to its shareholders on how it has taken the impact on key stakeholders into account when making decisions.

10. The board should provide feedback to those stakeholders with whom it has engaged, which should be tailored to the different stakeholder groups.

(The Stakeholder Voice in Board Decision Making)

Channels of communication with different stakeholder groups

Organisations can use many channels of communication today to assist them in stakeholder engagement. The most commonly used are as follows.

Investors

- Results presentations and roadshows
- Presentations at annual shareholder meetings
- Other management organised presentations on key issues important to the organisation
- Surveys.

Contractors and suppliers

- Commercial interactions
- Tender and contracting negotiations
- Compliance processes
- Open days
- Policy briefings
- Whistleblowing procedures.

Customers

- Commercial relationships
- Surveys
- Complaints procedures
- Open days
- Advertising
- Social media
- Whistleblowing procedures.

Governments

- Direct engagement
- Indirect engagement through:
  - industry associations
  - lobbying groups
  - bilateral organisations
  - organisations representing different interest groups.

Media

- Press briefings and releases
- Open days
- Presentations at annual shareholder meetings.

Communities

- Social responsibility plans
- Public forms and meetings
- Impact assessments
- Complaints procedures
- Whistleblowing procedures.

Trade unions

- Annual negotiations
- Meetings
- Presentations
- Whistleblowing procedures.

Employees

- Meetings
- Social media
- Employee advisor council
- Presentations
- Whistleblowing procedures.

NGOs and civil society organisations

- Reports
- Briefings
- Surveys
- Partnerships
- Impact assessments
- Engagement on industry-specific issues
- Memberships
- Social investment.

International organisations

- Membership of organisations such as UN Global Compact
- Human Rights organisations
- Industry-specific organisations such as the Extractive Industries Transparency Initiative (EITI) and International Council on Mining and Metals (ICMM) for mining organisations.

As we have seen earlier in this chapter, it is important for organisations to determine which method of communication is the most appropriate. Sometimes the most effective method is not the most appropriate. For example, an organisation once laid off some of its workforce by sending them SMS text messages. It was a very effective method of communication in that all the employees received the message. The subsequent press coverage, however, questioned whether it was the most appropriate method of communication for communicating this kind of news to employees.

Reporting on engagement with stakeholders

Organisations are increasingly reporting on their engagement with stakeholders. Whether or not an organisation has been able to implement what it has learned from a stakeholder, there appears to be an expectation that the organisation will report back either specifically or through a published report, giving recognition to the stakeholders' concerns.

Consideration should be given as to whether reporting on stakeholder engagement should be translated into local languages, especially if the engagement has been with a local community. The level of reporting should be pitched at the audience. There is no point developing sophisticated reporting tools if the stakeholder audience is illiterate or does not have access to those tools. An organisation may therefore have to develop several tiers of communication to cover all stakeholder group requirements.

The role of the company secretary

In many organisations, the board looks to the company secretary to assist them with stakeholder engagement. The company secretary can do this in several ways:

- Liaising with management to ensure that the board is advised on who the organisation's stakeholders are and what roles stakeholders can play in assisting the organisation in creating value and being sustainable in the long term.
- Explaining to the board the business case for stakeholder engagement.
- Assisting the board in adopting stakeholder engagement as a core corporate value and liaising with management to ensure that policies and plans are implemented to make sure that the organisation leverages the most out of its stakeholder engagement.
- Liaising with management to ensure that the board is advised how to engage with different stakeholder groups.
- Advising the board on reporting, ensuring that the management make recommendations for reporting to specific stakeholder groups and, where appropriate, developing reports to specific stakeholder groups.
- Working with the management, compliance officers and investor relations officers to ensure the correct strategies, policies and procedures are in place to manage the risks, especially reputational risk, and to take advantage of the opportunities presented by particular stakeholders.
- Advising the board on any reputational risk aspects to the company from any stakeholder or stakeholder group.

Chapter summary

- Organisations are not 'islands' and to ensure that they maintain a licence to operate, they need to engage with their stakeholders. This requires organisations to identify who their key stakeholders are and how to engage with them.

- The level of engagement with stakeholders may depend on an organisation's approach to governance. Those who adopt a stakeholder approach to governance will have a greater focus on stakeholder needs and interests.
- How organisations communicate with their stakeholders will depend on the type of stakeholder and the message to be communicated.
- Boards are required by best practice to develop policies and strategies for identifying and engaging with stakeholders in the most effective ways.

7 Corporate social responsibility and integrated reporting

Introduction

This chapter describes what is meant by corporate social responsibility and what drives organisations to be more socially responsible. It also considers how corporate social responsibility can be integrated into an organisation's strategy to achieve long-term sustainability for the organisation. The chapter also looks at how organisations are reporting on their corporate social responsibility activities.

Definition of corporate social responsibility

As with corporate governance, there appears to be no universally accepted definition of corporate social responsibility (CSR). (See 'Definitions of CSR' on page 130 for examples of some of the definitions.) As we will see in this chapter, some organisations understand it as pure charitable giving others as an integral part of their business models and hence include CSR activities as part of their strategic planning. Others combine their environmental activities with CSR. The type of involvement in CSR by organisations will depend on their operational activities, their understanding of CSR, and the philosophy and values of their organisation.

Various terms are used to describe CSR. These include: corporate citizenship, responsible business, sustainable responsible business, corporate social performance, corporate moral responsibility and corporate sustainability. In this chapter, we will refer to the concept as CSR.

CSR is not a new phenomenon. In the late eighteenth century and nineteenth century, following the Industrial Revolution in Britain, many entrepreneurs, including Robert Owen (New Lanark – cotton mills), the Lever Brothers (Port Sunlight – soap) and the Cadbury family (Bourneville – chocolate) developed what have become known as model villages around their factories, where workers had free housing, health care and education. These were the origins of corporate social responsibility, which aimed at ensuring a fit, healthy and sober workforce focused on production.

Some believe that following World War II, the advent of free education and the National Health Service in the UK saw the state take over from companies the responsibility for the well-being of the workforce. This in turn led to companies focusing more on making profits and achieving growth to help economic recovery after the war than on acting in the interests of society at large.

By the late 1980s, society was becoming more and more concerned with the behaviour of corporations and their lack of concern for the communities within which they operated. There was a belief by some that short-term profits were being focused on to the detriment of long-term profitability and sustainability, not just of the organisations but also of society as a whole. In 1991, a theoretical debate on 'doing well by doing good' was started by the Porter hypothesis that the financial benefits from innovation induced by CSR more than offset the engagement and compliance costs. There has also been a growing recognition since the early 1990s that the reputational impact of a good CSR rating is positive to an organisation as the outside world sees the organisation as decent, trustworthy and good to its employees, the community and the environment. Evidence shows that this increases the financial returns for an organisation's investors.

ResearchGate commissioned a study into whether CSR is linked to profitability. The study was based on CSR information available from the annual reports of Royal Dutch Shell Plc over a five-year period: 2001–05. The results of the study:

> … indicate that socially responsible corporate performance can be associated with profitability. Although this study did not explore the direction of the causal connections, nevertheless, the findings indicate that CSR is positively related to better financial performance (profitability) and this relationship is statistically significant.

Despite evidence of CSR's benefits to organisations, some sceptics of CSR claim that most organisations are involved in CSR because of what they expect to gain from it and question the motive behind CSR activities. They believe that the major motive behind the practice is advertisement or superficial window-dressing, as such activities are often accompanied by photo opportunities and publicity activities in the press. It has even been postulated that some organisations use CSR activities to cover up unethical or harmful practices that their core operations are involved in.

'Greenwashing' is the practice of making an unsubstantiated or misleading claim about the environmental benefits of a product, service, technology or company practice. An example of greenwashing is an organisation committing to reduce the environmental impact of its product line before the products are even ready.

An organisation's stakeholders, especially the media, will be looking out for organisations that are not delivering on the promises they make. If found out, organisations risk a drop in brand value and trust, loss of sales and, where those organisations are listed on a stock exchange, a drop in the share price.

DEFINITIONS OF CSR

The European Union has defined CSR as 'a concept whereby companies integrate social and environmental concerns in their business operations and in their interaction with their stakeholders on a voluntary basis'.

The World Business Council for Sustainable Development defined CSR as 'the continuing commitment by business to behave ethically and contribute to economic development while improving the quality of life of the workforce and their families as well as of the local community and society at large'.

King IV, the South African Corporate Governance Code, uses the term 'corporate citizenship' and defines it as 'the recognition that the organisation is an integral part of the broader society in which it operates, affording the organisation standing as a juristic person in that society with rights but also responsibilities and obligations. It is also a recognition that the broader society is the licensor of the organisation'.

CSR and corporate governance

Because of these reputational issues and the fact that CSR concerns an organisation's business operations and causes interaction with different stakeholder groups, including investors, CSR is linked to corporate governance. As we saw in Chapter 1 there are different approaches to corporate governance, and the view of CSR is very different depending on the approach that is taken.

Stakeholder approach

CSR is practised in the context of the stakeholder theory of corporate governance. As we saw in Chapter 1, this extends the scope of the corporate governance notion beyond the relationship between management and shareholders to include other relevant parties that have an interest in the operations of an organisation. The theory is premised on the concept of a company being a legal or artificial person that operates in a community, and on the view that there should be some explicit recognition of the well-being of other groups having a long-term association with the firm – and therefore an interest, or stake, in its long-term success.

Shareholder value approach

The shareholder value approach to corporate governance has the opposite view. This approach is based upon Milton Friedman's argument that a corporation's purpose is to maximise returns to its shareholders and not to have social responsibilities to society as a whole. Friedman stated the following regarding corporate social responsibility in his article that he published in the *New York Times* in the 1970s:

> When I hear businessmen speak eloquently about the 'social responsibilities of business in a free enterprise system,' I am reminded of the wonderful line about the Frenchman who discovered at the age of 70 that he had been speaking prose all his life. The businessmen believe that they are defending free enterprise when they declaim that business is not concerned 'merely' with profit but also with promoting desirable 'social' ends; that business has a 'social conscience' and takes seriously its responsibilities for providing employment, eliminating discrimination, avoiding pollution and whatever else may be the catchwords of the contemporary crop of reformers. In fact they are or would be if they or anyone else took them seriously preaching pure and unadulterated socialism. Businessmen who talk this way are unwitting puppets of the intellectual forces that have been undermining the basis of a free society these past decades.

Friedman believed that only people could have societal responsibilities; 'business' as a whole could not be said to have such responsibilities. He argued that organisations should act in accordance with the interests of their owners, which generally would be to make as much money as possible while complying with the law.

The organisation's primary responsibility was to shareholders, as enshrined in company laws worldwide. It was the responsibility of the individual shareholders, customers and employees themselves to choose whether to participate in CSR. It was, therefore, not the responsibility of companies to engage in CSR.

An alternative view

A different view was expressed by Ann Bernstein (2010). She proposed that just by being in business, organisations were conducting a CSR activity. She stated that 'sustained economic performance (rather than any other measure) should be the first dimension of good corporate citizenship'.

The Report emanating from the U.S. President's Commission on Industrial Competitiveness (March 1985) arrived at what seems to be a similar conclusion when it stated that an organisation, by producing products or services of superior quality or lower costs, was conducting CSR activities as it contributed to improving the quality of life of its stakeholders.

Bernstein provided two examples of where multinationals created a large social impact through their existence alone. The first is the Coca-Cola Company when it commenced operations in China, and the second is the impact of Microsoft.

CASE STUDY: COCA-COLA COMPANY IN CHINA

Coca-Cola uses a franchise model whereby it sells concentrate to bottling companies worldwide. Coca-Cola continues to manage the overall brand strategy, including research and development. The bottling partners handle merchandising and distribution locally.

Ann Bernstein (2010) used the following study by Peking University, Tsinghua University, and the University of Carolina to show the impact on the Chinese economy of Coca-Cola entering the market. Their findings can be summarised as follows:

- Coca-Cola employed 14,046 people. More than 62% were skilled workers, most of whom were permanently employed. Some 350,000 people were employed in the bottling system, and the sale of Coca-Cola products supported 50,000 jobs in wholesale and retail sectors.

- About 414,000 direct and indirect jobs were sustained by Coca-Cola's production and distribution in China.
- In 1998, Coca-Cola injected 8.16 billion RMB into the Chinese economy, generating additional Chinese output of about 21.7 billion RMB.
- Also in 1998, Coca-Cola paid 387 million RMB in taxes to the Chinese government.
- The additional economic activity stimulated by Coca-Cola's activities generated an additional 1.2 billion RMB in tax (Peking University et al., 2000).

Coca-Cola has thus had qualitative effects on the Chinese economy. Managers of bottling plants are financially accountable, have instituted better inventory and quality control, and cost management systems and routinely track consumer preferences, and pay attention to their product's distribution. Workers are rewarded for hard work.

Cola-Cola has stimulated small business. On average, 28% of the owners of retail shops and restaurants in Harbin, Guangdong province, Shanghai, and Xian were jobless before starting their ventures. Many subsequently depended on selling Coca-Cola products for their livelihood.

Coca-Cola has also contributed to more substantial business development. For example, in 1986 the Zhong Fu Industrial Group began to follow Coca-Cola, setting up bottle-making plants near every new Coca-Cola plant. By 1999, Zhong Fu had 36 plants across the country, and began to export bottles to Japan and South East Asia (Peking University et al., 2000).

Lastly, Coca-Cola has helped to strengthen Chinese markets by providing training to tens of thousands of Chinese and by investing its capital and experience in developing localised soft-drink brands.

Coca-Cola has continued to invest in China with subsequent impact on the economy. In 2009, Coca-Cola opened an Innovation and Technology Centre in Shanghai at a cost of $90 million. China provides the second largest number of science and engineering graduates in the world. This centre hopes to leverage of this by providing employment to some of these graduates.

In 2010, Coca-Cola announced its corporate objectives for China, which included:

- increasing sales there by 15% by 2015; and
- establishing three new manufacturing firms in rural areas.

Both objectives would lead to further direct and indirect income generation and job creation in China.

CASE STUDY: MICROSOFT

Microsoft carried out a study of the half a million or so companies worldwide, selling or servicing its products: PCs and servers; software vendors; retail outlet and resellers; and training firms. Microsoft refers to these companies, many of which are small local firms, as its ecosystem.

In 2007, 42% of the 354 million people in the global IT sector were employed by the Microsoft ecosystem, generating some $514 billion in taxes. For every dollar that Microsoft made in 2007, the ecosystem made $7.79.

The study showed that Microsoft has had an enormous impact on job creation, revenue generation, and business opportunity and that this is likely to continue with the creation of more than 100,000 new businesses in the IT market between 2007 and 2011. Many of these companies will be small and locally owned.

(Extracted from Ann Bernstein (2010), *The Case for Business in Developing Countries*, Penguin Books)

Corporate social responsibility through the decades

The CSR focus of organisations has changed through the decades since 1990. Figure 7.1, sets out what topics were the main focus in which decade.

	Economic	Social	Environmental
1990s		• occupational health & safety • community development health & safety • HIV/AIDS	
2000s	• ethical business practices • industry codes & standards • energy efficiency	• human rights • corporate social investment • employee wellness	• environmental protection • water security • biodiversity • climate change
2010s	• integrated thinking, reporting and risk management		• Green Growth

Figure 7.1: CSR through the decades

The focus has been driven from three different sources: the organisations themselves, governments and bilateral organisations, and investors.

Organisations themselves

KPMG has carried out global surveys on why organisations carry out and report on CSR activities. The results of the 2005–11 surveys are set out in Figure 7.2. Interestingly, the 2015 survey cited government/legal requirements as the main reason for reporting.

Driver	2005	2008	2011
Reputation or Brand	27%	55%	67%
Ethical considerations	53%	69%	58%
Innovation and Learning	53%	55%	44%
Employee Motivation	47%	52%	44%
Risk Management or Reduction	47%	35%	35%
Access to capital/increased s/h value	39%	29%	32%
Economic considerations	74%	68%	32%
Strengthened supplier relationships	13%	32%	22%
Market position improvement	21%	22%	22%
Improved relations with Govt.	9%	21%	18%
Cost Savings	9%	17%	10%

Figure 7.2: CSR reporting

Organisations have also realised that they can use CSR activities for the following:
- To obtain competitive advantage. For example:
  - Cadbury announced that all cocoa in Dairy Milk chocolate would be certified by Fairtrade.
  - BP, in the late 1990s, committed the company to reducing its emissions of greenhouse gases that contributed to global warming. The initial process cost to BP was about $20 million but by 2007 the company had saved $2 billion.
  - In 2002, Unilever commenced a five-year programme, Swasthya Chetna, in Indian rural communities aimed at hygiene education.

Working in partnership with parents, health educators, teachers, community leaders and government agencies, the aim was to educate 20% of the population (200 million people) about basic hygiene habits, including washing hands with soap. In 2005, sales of Lifebuoy soap in India increased by 10%.

- To reduce risk, especially reputational risk. However, as we shall see later, organisations should use these activities not to cover up wrongdoing, which may antagonise stakeholders, but to help mitigate the risks or prevent them from happening.

- To attract human capital. Evidence seems to suggest that organisations that have a strong reputation for pursuing CSR activities find it easier to attract and retain talented employees. This is more relevant with the millennial generation. Employees also seem to perform better in organisations pursuing CSR policies.

- For innovation. Mobile phone banking in Africa was developed originally by Vodafone for Safaricom, a Kenyan-based telecommunications company, in 2007 to provide individuals in rural areas with money transfer, financing and microfinancing services. The idea came from research funded by the Department of International Development (DFID), in 2002, at Gamos and the Commonwealth Telecommunications Organisation. They documented that in Uganda, Botswana and Ghana, people were spontaneously using airtime as a proxy for money transfer.

- For sustainability. The shift in thinking by many in the corporate world to long-term thinking has led to a realisation that to be sustainable, an organisation has to focus more on its CSR activities, which are seen to be vital for the long-term sustainability of the organisation. When defining their strategies, organisations have to consider the challenge of sourcing the different resources they need, recognising that these resources are becoming scarcer and hence more expensive. This challenge is only going to get worse in future years. Pressure is on organisations to therefore to develop strategies for utilising their resources more effectively and efficiently. This pressure has led to more and more organisations adopting the concept of 'integrated thinking' as part of their strategy development.

Integrated thinking is a process that takes into consideration in a balanced way the effective and efficient utilisation of each of the following six capital resources available to an organisation when developing strategy or decision making.

- **Financial capital** – money, equity, bonds, monetary value of assets, etc. that an organisation needs to operate.
- **Human capital** – the collective skills and experience of the people that work for the organisation.
- **Manufactured capital** – physical means and infrastructure needed for an organisation to provide its products and services, e.g. fixed assets.
- **Intellectual capital** – patents, copyright, designs, goodwill, brand value and knowledge accumulated, i.e. intangible assets.
- **Natural capital** – natural resources and energy that the organisation depends on to produce its products/services.
- **Social capital** – value added to an organisation of the social relationships with individuals and institutions that an organisation has developed through its stakeholder engagement.

For organisations to have effective integrated thinking, they need information about how effectively they are using the above types of capital. This information is provided through 'integrated reporting', which will be discussed later in the chapter.

Governments and bilateral organisations

The governments of many countries have become interested in CSR due to the pressure from their citizens to protect the environment and improve the quality of life for those citizens, and for companies to take responsibility for the impacts of their business. The governments need to balance this desire of their citizens with economic success. Laws and regulatory requirements have therefore been introduced in many countries to set minimum standards for the protection of the environment and society at large. Examples of such laws and regulations include environmental, health and safety at work, protection of employee rights, the UK Modern Slavery Act, payment practices reporting, consumer rights and anti-discrimination (gender, race, religion, sexual preference or age), among others.

The Organisation for Economic Co-operation and Development has issued guidelines for multinationals on sustainable development, human rights, employee rights, human capital development, compliance with laws and regulations, and protection of the environment.

The World Bank Group, including the International Finance Corporation and the United Nations, has also issued guidance in areas such as human rights and good corporate governance practices. These include social and environmental practices as good corporate citizens.

Investors

Many investors recognise the impact of CSR issues on success and therefore take a company's CSR practices into consideration in their investment decision making. Factors such as the company's record on human rights, child labour, impact of the company's activities on the environment, and the nature of business are taken into account. Some investors would not invest in companies whose practices are considered to go against the values espoused by the investors or to be violating laws, regulations and the principles of human rights. This also includes any products that are considered harmful to society, such as tobacco, arms and ammunitions.

Shareholder trade associations

Many shareholder trade associations have issued guidance on socially responsible investment for their members. These include, among others:

- UK – Pensions and Lifetime Savings Association (formerly NAPF);
- UK – Investment Association (formerly ABI and IMA);
- US – CalPERS, which has integrated since 2011 environmental, social and governance issues into its investment decision making; and
- International Corporate Governance Network (ICGN), which issued its Global Stewardship Principles in 2016.

Some countries have introduced Indexes to rank organisations on their CSR activities – for example, the FTSE 4 Good Indices in the UK and the Dow Jones Sustainability Indices in the USA.

The focus on an organisation's CSR activities has grown over recent years. One of the main reasons for this appears to be the millennium generation entering the workplace. Millennials want to be heard and have a voice in both contributing and making a difference in a broader community. They constantly share their views and opinions through social media – twitter, Facebook, YouTube, etc. This characteristic of the millennial generation has led to an overwhelming demand for CSR as the potential workforce and consumer base look to do business only with those whom they feel are making a positive impact on society and pillorying those through social media who appear to be negatively impacting society. According to a 2015 Cone Communications Millennial CSR Study, 'more than 9 in 10 millennials would switch brands to one associated with a cause' and take a pay cut to work for a responsible organisation (see Table 7.1).

Table 7.1: 2015 Cone Communications Millennial CSR Study

Action	% millennials	% general population
Switch brands to one associated with a cause	91	85
Use social media to engage around CSR	66	53
Purchase a product with a social or environmental benefit	87	83
Tell friends and family about CSR efforts	82	72
Voice opinions to a company about its CSR efforts	70	60
Volunteer for a cause supported by a company they trust	74	56
Pay more for a product to have an impact on issues they care about	70	66
Share products rather than buying to have an impact on issues they care about	66	56
Take a pay cut to work for a responsible company	62	56
Use social media to share positive information about companies and issues they care about	38	30
Use social media to learn more about specific companies and issues	33	27
Use social media to share negative information about companies and issues they care about	26	21
Use social media to communicate directly with companies about issues	18	14
Use social media to contribute directly to an effort led by a company	17	12

Categories of corporate social responsibility activity

This section looks at the different categories of CSR activity and how companies are participating in CSR.

Different categories of CSR activity

Figure 7.3 shows the four main categories of CSR. It is based on a McKinsey article written by Keys *et al.* (2009).

Figure 7.3: The CSR landscape

Pet projects

These are the projects most closely associated worldwide with CSR. They frequently reflect the personal interests of board members or senior executives within the organisation. These activities often get a lot of press coverage for the organisation, but usually offer minimal benefits to society or the organisation. They are also very dependent on the individual whose interest it is for their sustainability. In hard times, these projects are often the first to be dropped, as their value to the organisation is low. Examples of such projects are sponsoring an art exhibition, a local theatre production, a local sports club event, etc.

Philanthropy

Philanthropy usually takes the form of large charitable donations to groups of people, institutions or individuals. These donations can be in the form of money, equipment and other materials, or even staff time where the company has the expertise to assist others who need their input. Examples of these activities include large donations to charitable organisations, educational projects, health care projects, scholarships for students who cannot afford to pay their fees and sponsorships for needy people to receive medical attention. This category of CSR activities confers the majority of the benefit on society. There is often little noise and fanfare with these donations and therefore often questionable reputational benefits to the organisation.

Propaganda

Activities in this category are focused primarily on building the organisation's reputation. They have little real benefit to society. They include sponsoring large sporting events, renovating and covering properties in advertising, sponsoring an international event, etc.

Organisations need to be careful when pursuing this category of CSR activities. If it is perceived that there is a gap between the organisation's words and actions, this may be dangerous to the reputation of the organisation.

Partnerships

CSR activities that create significant shared value creation for both the organisation and society fall within the category of partnerships. Such activities usually create value for the organisation by addressing major strategic issues or challenges faced by the organisation. This in turn leads to a long-term sustainable benefit for society, as it is in the best interests of the organisation to continue the activity. It makes business sense.

Examples of organisations' CSR activities are as follows.

EXAMPLES OF CORPORATE SOCIAL RESPONSIBILITY PARTNERSHIPS

Satemwa and Médecins Sans Frontières
Satemwa in Malawi is a certified Fair Trade producer of tea. HIV was having a negative impact on the company, and the in-house clinical services on the estate were insufficient. Satemwa therefore entered into a partnership with Médecins Sans Frontières for the provision of voluntary counselling and testing (VCT) services to employees and local communities.

Unilever and Dove
In 2004, Unilever created the Dove Self-Esteem Project (DSEP). This project was aimed at helping girls and young women to develop a positive relationship with the way they looked. The project has helped millions of young people around the world to build body confidence and self-esteem. By

---

2015, the project had reached 20 million young people. Unilever/Dove aims to reach another 20 million by 2020.

The DSEP includes the following components:

- 'Confident Me', a series of courses for teachers to conduct in schools;
- 'Uniquely Me', for parents to discuss with girls of all ages; and
- 'True to Me', a step-by-step activity guide for youth leaders and mentors to encourage mindfulness with girls aged 10–14.

As part of the DSEP, Unilever/Dove has partnered with the girl guides and girl scouts associations with the aim of reaching 3.5 million girls across 125 countries by the end of 2016. The programme is to be extended from 2017 to 2020, with an aim of reaching an additional 3 million girls.

In 2016, Unilever/Dove expanded their formal education reach by partnering with the governments of France, Argentina and the UK to disseminate self-esteem education in schools.

Unilever's data shows that as well as raising awareness about body confidence, the project has helped to 'drive Dove loyalty and growth'.

Unilever and the World Wildlife Fund

In the mid-1990s, Unilever realised that its supply of fish for its fish fingers was at risk. In partnership with the World Wildlife Fund, the company set up the Marine Stewardship Council, an independent body to promote sustainable fisheries around the world. The Council certifies fisheries that limit the total catch. To create incentives for fishermen to seek certification, Unilever committed to buying 100% of its fish from sustainable sources.

Walmart and Patagonia

Walmart has partnered with Yvon Chouinard, the Founder of Patagonia, the outdoor-clothing brand. The two companies have created the Sustainable Apparel Coalition, inviting other major brands, such as Levi Strauss, Nike, Gap and Adidas to join them in crafting clear, quantifiable standards for environmentally responsible clothing production.

Creating CSR partnerships

In July 2004, Marco Albani and Kimberly Henderson published the findings of their research into what makes partnership collaborations work long term. They identified the following seven essential principles:

1. Identify clear reasons to collaborate – when choosing a partner or agreeing to enter into a partnership, it is important for both organisations to understand why they are collaborating and identify strong incentives for the partnership. Entering a partnership just

because you don't want to be left out is not a good reason and will usually lead to a weak partnership.

2. Find a 'fairy godmother' – it is important for both organisations to identify a core group of people totally committed to the partnership. There is often a lot of risk associated with getting these partnerships started, so commitment to the cause is essential.

3. Set simple, credible goals – it is important for the organisation to have a simple goal achievable goal especially where the partners are unlikely bedfellows. For example, Unilever and the World Wildlife Fund (WWF) had different motives for collaborating in the Marine Stewardship Council (MSC) but the same objective: ensuring sustainable fish stocks. Unilever at the time was the world's largest fish retailer. The WWF received a lot of criticism for collaborating with a multinational. It was seen as compromising their values by other NGOs.

4. Get professional help – most partnerships need help to get started, especially where the cultures of the organisations clash, for example a private sector organisation and NGO. The facilitator should be independent and be able to drive the project forward especially at the start while the partner organisations are getting set up for the project. As the project matures, it may be possible to phase out a facilitator.

5. Dedicate good people to the cause – if the partnership is seen to be strategic, both organisations will dedicate good people to the collaboration. Tying incentives and career progression to the success of the partnership is also important in ensuring that it is successful.

6. Be flexible in defining success – don't be too ambitious in what you are trying to achieve, as projects often depend on many issues to succeed. Achieving something may be moving in the right direction. The first time Unilever disclosed its environmental targets, it disclosed that it had not met all the targets but had made progress towards them. The organisation received a lot of kudos for trying and what it had achieved, and virtually no criticism for not having achieved the targets.

7. Prepare to let go – organisations should plan an exit strategy for the partnership. It may be winding down the project or spinning it off into a separate organisation.

Some organisations are starting to use CSR targets or achieving a certain status on a CSR Index as part of the performance criteria in bonus and incentive schemes for senior executives. For example, Royal Dutch Shell (RDS), which has been reporting on its environmental and social performance since 1997, tracks a range of environmental and social indicators. It has also established an external review committee of independent experts to help the organisation evaluate and improve the quality and credibility of its sustainability reporting.

CSR reporting

An important part of good governance is good reporting. Companies have been reporting their financial information for well over 100 years. The way in which they are required to report this information is heavily regulated. Over the last 15 years or so, organisations have started to report on non-financial information.

Supporters of non-financial reporting feel that the addition of this reporting provides a broader, more meaningful understanding of the organisation's business, and its impact on the environment and the society where it operates. It also helps stakeholders understand the organisation's strategy and risk management.

The major players demanding that organisations report on the economic, social and environmental impact of their operations are:

- shareholders/investors;
- governments;
- consumers;
- other businesses, such as suppliers;
- employees;
- banks;
- insurance companies;
- stock market analysts if the company is listed; and
- social and environmental activists.

Most of this reporting has been voluntary.

Drivers for voluntary CSR reporting

Some of the reasons for this voluntary reporting were discussed earlier – for example, the impact of the millennial generation. There are, however, other important drivers of CSR reporting. These include:

- a greater requirement for accountability from stakeholders has been important in encouraging organisations to report voluntarily on their CSR activities and on their impact on the environment and societies in which we live. Voluntary industry initiative requirements include the UN Global Compact, Global Reporting Initiative (GRI), Principles for Responsible Investment (PRI) etc.;
- stakeholder pressure groups – NGOs such as World Wildlife Fund, Greenpeace, Friends of the Earth, etc.; and
- financiers and regulators (the Equator Principles).

Statutory and listing requirements

Many countries are now introducing some form of mandatory non-financial reporting. This is because there has been a recognition that financial reporting tells only half the story. In the UK, the Companies Act 2006 includes requirements for quoted companies to report on the following social and environmental issues in their strategy report:

- environmental matters (including the impact of the company's business on the environment);
- the company's employees; and
- social, community and human rights issues.

Other examples are the US Sarbanes Oxley Act 2002, the Paris Accord and Kyoto Protocol on climate change, and the European Union, which has developed a series of directives, including:

- Restriction of Hazardous Substances Directive (RoHS);
- Waste Electrical and Electronic Equipment Directive (WEEE);
- Directive on Registration, Evaluation and Authorization of Chemicals (REACH); and
- Non-Financial Reporting Directive.

Organisations present their non-financial information as part of their annual report, either in a separate CSR report or in an integrated report. Whichever method is chosen, it is important for organisations to develop and track metrics (both relative and absolute), as with financial information. Reporting can be in hard-copy annual reports or online through organisational websites. Unilever's online *Sustainable Living Report*, which can be found on the Unilever website, is a good example.

Global Reporting Initiative sustainability reporting framework

The Global Reporting Initiative (GRI) is one of the most popular reporting frameworks. The GRI framework comprises a set of core principles to guide organisations in selecting and compiling information, and developing the underlying systems for ongoing, effective management of the environmental, social and economic aspects of their operations. It also includes a set of standard corporate disclosures and specific performance indicators to various industries that have been developed and are continuously improved through a vigorous and ongoing multi-stakeholder process. More information on GRI can be found at www.global-reporting.org.

Integrated reporting

The greater desire for accountability by an organisation's stakeholders has led to the development of the concept of integrated reporting.

The South African Corporate Governance Code was the first to include provisions on integrated reporting in King III in 2009. Since then the understanding of the concept has evolved. The latest version, King IV, defines integrated reporting as 'a process founded on integrated thinking that results in a periodic integrated report by an organisation about value creation over time. It includes related communications regarding aspects of value creation.' An integrated report is defined as 'a concise communication about how an organisation's strategy, governance, performance and prospects, in the context of its external environment, lead to the creation of value in the short, medium and long-term'. King III had stated that 'integrated reporting' reflected the challenge that organisations faced to make sustainability issues mainstream in their operations and to integrate social, environmental and economic issues into the way that the organisation operates. King IV assumes that sustainability issues are now mainstream for most organisations and that integrated reporting is an outcome of integrated thinking by the organisation's governing body.

The economic value of a company includes its balance sheet and profit and loss statement, an assessment of future earnings, brand, goodwill, the quality of its board and management, reputation, strategy and other sustainability aspects. All of these elements are found in an integrated report. Integrated reporting is, therefore, seen as essential to enable all stakeholders (internal and external) to make informed assessments of the economic value of a company.

The integrated report should record how the company has impacted (both positively and negatively) the economic life of the community in which it operated during the year, and how in the coming year it can improve the positive and eradicate or reduce the negative aspects.

Principle 5 of King IV states: 'The governing body should ensure that all reports issued by the organisation enable stakeholders to make informed assessments of the organisation's performance, and its short, medium and long-term prospects.' Recommended practice 12 under this principle goes on to say:

> The governing body should oversee that the organisation issues an integrated report at least annually, which is either:
> - A standalone report which connects the more detailed information in other reports and addresses, at a high level and in a complete, concise way, the matters that could significantly affect the organisation's ability to create value; or
> - A distinguishable, prominent and accessible part of another report which also includes the annual financial statements and other reports which must be issued in compliance with legal provisions.

In August 2009, His Royal Highness the Prince of Wales, through his Accounting for Sustainability Project (A4S) convened a meeting of investors, standard setters, companies, accounting bodies and UN representatives, which established the International Integrated Reporting Committee. The Committee was chaired by Mervyn King, the namesake of the King Reports. The Committee's purpose was to oversee the creation of a globally accepted integrated reporting framework. In 2011, the International Integrated Reporting Committee was renamed the International Integrated Reporting Council (IIRC).

IIRC integrated reporting framework

The IIRC has developed an international integrated reporting framework and issued guidance on integrated reporting in an attempt to build consensus among governments, listing authorities, businesses, investors and accounting bodies on the future shape of corporate reporting.

The IIRC 2013 guidance on integrated reporting establishes guiding principles and content elements for an integrated report. It does not set benchmarks for assessing such things as the quality of the organisation strategy or the level of its performance. This is because assessments of this kind are the role of the report user, based on the information provided by the company in its integrated report.

The IIRC guiding principles are:

- strategic focus and future orientation;
- connectivity of information;
- responsiveness and stakeholder inclusiveness;
- materiality and conciseness;
- reliability; and
- comparability and consistency.

The IIRC content elements for an integrated report are:

- organisational overview and business model;
- operating context, including risks and opportunities;
- strategic objectives and strategies;
- governance and remuneration;
- performance; and
- future outlook.

These content elements are not mutually exclusive and are fundamentally linked to each other. How a company presents the information in the integrated report should show this interconnectedness, rather than presenting the information in standalone 'silos'. Historically information has often been reported by department or function and it is therefore difficult to assess the impact of one area on another in the organisation. According to the IIRC, integrated reporting should lead to a more accurate picture about what is going on in an organisation. This is turn should:

- promote change in corporate behaviour, decision making and thinking with a focus on long-term, in addition to medium- and short-term, value creation and preservation;
- inform resource allocation by investors, again creating a focus on long-term as well as the short- and medium-term value creation and preservation;
- catalyse a more cohesive and comprehensive approach to corporate reporting that communicates the full range of factors that materially affect the ability of an organisation to create and preserve value over time; and

- enhance accountability and stewardship with respect to a broader base of capitals than just financial capital (including manufactured, human intellectual, natural and social [and relationship] capitals) and promote understanding of the interdependencies between them.

According to the IIRC there are, at the time of writing, 1,500 businesses worldwide using integrated reporting to communicate with their investors, 300 businesses of which are in Japan. Regulators in Japan, India and the UK are among those taking a greater interest in integrated reporting as a route towards more cohesive reporting and financial stability.

The importance of 'integrated thinking' to integrated reporting

As discussed previously, 'integrated thinking' is important to integrated reporting as this enables an organisation to understand better the relationships between its various operating and functional units and the capitals the organisation uses and affects. Integrated thinking should take into account the connectivity and interdependencies between all those factors that have a material effect on an organisation's ability to create and preserve value in the short, medium and long term, including (but not limited to):

- the capitals the organisation uses and affects, including the critical interdependencies of financial, manufactured, human, intellectual, natural and social capitals;
- the external context in which the organisation operates;
- the opportunities and risks faced by the organisation and how it tailors its strategies to manage them;
- activities, results and performance – past, present and future; and
- financial and non-financial information.

An integrated report should enhance transparency and accountability, which are essential in building trust and resilience, by disclosing:

- the nature and quality of the organisation's relationships with key stakeholders, such as customers, suppliers, employees and local communities; and
- how their issues are understood, taken into account and responded to.

Responding to stakeholder issues

An integrated report should show how an organisation is responding to stakeholder issues. How organisations respond to stakeholder issues is demonstrated through decisions, actions and performance, as well as ongoing communication with stakeholders. An integrated report is an important part of the communication process with stakeholders. This does not mean that the report should attempt to satisfy all the information needs of all stakeholders. Rather, by focusing on matters that are most material to long-term success, an integrated report will often provide relevant information in itself, as well as a clear reference point for other communications, including compliance information, investor presentations, detailed financial information, sustainability reports and communications directed to specific stakeholders who have particular information needs. Much of this more detailed information is likely to be placed online.

One integrated report

In the introduction to Philips' 'Annual Report 2008: Financial, Social and Environmental Performance', the organisation explained why it had combined all of the financial, social and environmental information into a single report. In summary, the two main reasons were as follows:

- It is a key element of taking sustainability seriously. An organisation should create a truly sustainable strategy responding to the risks and opportunities created by the need to ensure a sustainable society. One this has been achieved the only way to report on it is in an integrated fashion. To try to split it back into 'silos' of financial and non-financial information does not make business sense.
- One report can give a single simplified message to an organisation's stakeholders. It helps improve transparency in corporate reporting.

Eccles and Krzus (2010) describe the four major benefits to an organisation which has adopted integrated reporting:

1. *Greater clarity about relationships and commitments*
   Integrated reporting helps companies identify the most important financial and non-financial metrics for the company. Management is also able to describe what it believes the relationship between financial and non-financial metrics should be. Most companies still have a lot of work to do on this. A 2008 KPMG CSR survey found

that only 16% of the G250 companies had quantified the value of corporate responsibility for their analyst and investor stakeholders. As management develops a better understanding of the relationships between financial and non-financial performance, it can re-evaluate what is included in its categories of risks, opportunities and choices. This will lead to better decisions.

2. *Better decisions*

As management attempts to be more explicit about the relationships between financial and non-financial outcomes, integrated reporting will help management strengthen or develop better metrics. In some cases, better information comes from simply combining data that already exists in the firm but may be being collected in different parts of the business. Kaplan and Norton's work on the Balanced Scorecard provides compelling evidence for how better measurement leads to better management decisions.

Also, when information is reported externally, the standards for its reliability are especially high. The higher-quality metrics required for external reporting demand higher-quality internal information, and this results in higher-quality decisions. The external transparency of the results of these decisions adds an incentive for making them good ones.

3. *Deeper engagement with all stakeholders*

In today's world, where companies are facing the demands of many stakeholders, it is essential that every stakeholder understands how its interests are related to those of others and to the factors that contribute to the level of performance that is being met. Integrated reporting therefore helps both companies and stakeholders take a more integrated view about how their interest relates to those of others.

Integrated reporting also helps eliminate the artificial distinction between shareholders and stakeholders. It can help shareholders focus in a more holistic way on a company's ability to earn profits and grow in the long term. A single integrated report ensures that there is a coherent and consistent message going out to all stakeholders. It creates a platform for one conversation in which all stakeholders can participate.

Through engagement, companies remain aware of the interests of their different stakeholders and how those interests are in alignment or conflict with each other. Companies should also encourage engagement among their stakeholders so that consensus can be reached on society's expectations for the company.

4. *Lower reputational risk*

An integrated view of the company's financial and non-financial performance, it is argued, will help identify areas at risk, since it will make clearer the areas where company's reputation is based on overlapping performance outcomes. It can also help companies monitor trends, social attitudes and the media and so improve awareness of how social norms and values are changing, helping the company become more aware of early-stage changes in expectations that will become more widely held and supported in the future.

Chapter summary

- Organisations face an increasing pressure to conduct their operations in a socially and environmentally friendly manner. This pressure is likely to continue with the millennial generation entering the workplace.
- Evidence shows that organisations that integrate their CSR activities into their business model and strategies have higher performance and are more likely to be sustainable.
- Many benefits of carrying out CSR activities comes from communicating their impact to stakeholders. This has led organisations to focus on CSR reporting.
- Traditionally CSR reporting was voluntary, but more countries are now introducing mandatory requirements.
- The integration of CSR activities into an organisation's business model and strategies has led to the integration of both financial and non-financial information in reporting – this is known as integrated reporting.

8　Governance and ethics

Introduction

There is a tendency to think that legal, regulatory and other responses to governance failures including criminal and civil prosecution of the culprits will deter wrongdoing. History has shown that this is not the case and has taught us that ethics is central to governance. This chapter explains the link between governance and ethics and explains how organisations can create an ethical culture.

> Good corporate governance has its foundation in effective & ethical leadership. Effective leadership is about directing performance and it is results driven… Ethical leadership is exemplified by responsibility, accountability, fairness & transparency. Ethical leadership & effective leadership should reinforce each other.
>
> (King IV Code of Corporate Governance)

The corporate scandals in the United Kingdom in the 1990s (such as Maxwell and Barrings Bank) and the corporate scandals in the United States (such as Enron and World Com) gave heightened attention to corporate failures and led to various interventions aimed at improving governance in organisations. However, it is important to note that corporate failures have existed for as long as organisations have been with us. The events of the 1990s and early 2000 are not the starting point. What gave those events prominence is a combination of factors that include media coverage that enabled the world to learn about them and the impact of those failures including loss of investor confidence, job losses, and corporate collapse among others. The response to those failures was a global dialogue on corporate failures that continues to date. One notable factor is that central to these failures are matters to do with governance and ethics.

This chapter seeks to explain the link between corporate governance and ethics, and explains the concepts of business ethics, ethical leadership and creating an ethical culture in organisations.

What is ethics?

It is difficult to define ethics succinctly. One might say ethics is synonymous with values such as honesty, integrity and accountability. These are corporate governance principles and core components of an ethical framework or ethical culture. Ogoola (2014) explains the difficulty in defining ethics and describes the concept of ethics:

> Fortunately, or unfortunately, some concepts are infinitely impervious to definition. Such concepts are simply too complex to be capable of simplistic definition…. Even that Goliath of moral philosophy Aristotle tried a definition of Ethics. He ended at making a distinction between virtue and vice: the one, a positive; and the other, a negative aspect of human behavior. Suffice to say that everyone knows Ethics, when they see it; when they smell it; when they hear it; when they taste it; and when they touch it. Equally, all know the opposite of Ethics (the Un-ethical), when they confront it, even at first glance. The one (the ethical) is a wholesome, positive force in societies, and, especially so, in the governance mechanisms of our societies. The others (the unethical) are stubborn, troublesome and totally negative forces, which must have absolutely no pride of place in the lawyer's professional kitty. Even though we may not be able to define the word 'Ethics' with any measure of exactitude, the concept of Ethics is self-evident. The concept has telltale sign posts which, when we pass them on our life's journey, ring a shrill bell to jolt our brain, to jerk our mind, and to twitch our conscience as to what animal we are passing. These signposts are many, and they are real. They include such signs as nobility, accountability, honesty, honour, trust, truth, openness, hard work, resilience, competence, diligence, proficiency, perseverance, charity, sacrifice, selflessness, self-denial and self-esteem. These, and others of their kind, in manifold array, are the constitutive elements that are integral to the chemical formula of the natural compound called Ethics.

(Ogoola, 2014)

It is very easy to think about ethics in the context of professionals such as doctors, lawyers and accountants. However, ethics is at the core of how individuals and organisations operate. It is at the core of how internal stakeholders within an organisation relate to each other and how the organisation relates to its external stakeholders. The challenges today in society that manifest themselves in social strife, professional misconduct and bad business practices occur largely as a result of unethical conduct.

Business ethics

The concept of business ethics is as old as business and pre-dates any form of business regulation as we understand it today. Business relationships were built on trust, fairness and respect, and therefore ethics cannot be divorced from business. These values were more pronounced in business relationships among close communities and were gradually watered down and replaced with business regulation (such as contract and securities regulation) as business relationships become impersonal and at arm's-length. One might argue that ethics is more important in arm's-length transactions, but there is a perception that business relationships are better governed by predictable and enforceable legal rules and this is evidenced by the wide ranging legal and regulatory frameworks that seek to protect various stakeholders in business including owners, providers of capital, investors, suppliers, employees and consumers.

The development of legal and regulatory frameworks to govern business may have created a perception that ethics is secondary to business and this is premised on the assumption that legal and regulatory frameworks are sufficient or even superior to ethical principles in guiding business behaviour. This has proved to be a misconception because unethical conduct has been at the heart of business failures and the resulting economic impacts despite heavy investment into improved legal and regulatory frameworks and enforcement. Therefore, ethics cannot be divorced from business.

Defining business ethics

Business ethics is the application of ethical values to business behaviour. Business ethics is relevant both to the conduct of individuals and to the conduct of the organisation as a whole. It applies to any and all aspects of business conduct, from boardroom strategies and how companies treat their employees and suppliers to sales techniques and accounting practices.

Ethics goes beyond the legal requirements for a company and is, therefore, about discretionary decisions and behaviour guided by values.

(Institute of Business Ethics)

Businesses usually have a set of core values usually stated on the website and other business documents. Therefore, business ethics is the application of core values in the day-to-day operations of the business. Commonly stated values include integrity, openness, social responsibility, fairness and respect.

The above principles apply internally and externally. For example, organisations are expected to treat employees fairly through policies and have policies that prevent discrimination at work, transparent recruitment processes and fair remuneration policies. The principle of fairness also applies to relationships with external stakeholders, such as suppliers, contractors, clients or customers.

It is common practice for organisations to have publicly stated core values and to state that these guide their approach to doing business. The values should also guide the way organisations relate with stakeholders including clients, suppliers, shareholders, financiers among others. Table 8.1 identifies core values of leading global brands.

Table 8.1: Core values of leading global brands

Organisation	Core values
Unilever	The organisations corporate success statement links success of the organisation to behaviour towards people, communities and the environment. Unilever's four core values are **integrity, responsibility, respect and pioneering.**
Cocoa- Cola	Cocoa-cola presents values as the guiding campus for the organisation's behaviour. The organisation's values are leadership, collaboration, integrity, accountability, passion, diversity, and quality.
Toyota	Toyota's global vision is to lead the future of mobility through safe and responsible ways of moving people. Toyota uses the metaphor of the tree to symbolise its vision where the key principles of the organisation provide the foundation for growth. These are fairness, respect, safety, productivity, innovation, trust and partnership.

There are interesting observations about the narratives on core values. They guide relationships and decision making, and influence behaviour. The narrative also points to positive outcomes of ethical business such as value creation, sustainability, innovation and productivity, and social and environmental impacts. Table 8.2 illustrates the application of ethical values to business behaviour.

Table 8.2: Application of ethical values to business behaviour

Value	Application
Integrity	• Culture of zero tolerance to corruption • Transparent procurement processes • Supply chain management
Openness	• Fair and accurate disclosure of information about products • Disclosure of financial information • Disclosure or material adverse information and remedial action
Social responsibility	• Assessment of environmental impacts of business and putting in place measures to mitigate negative impacts • Assessment of adverse social impacts of business, e.g. alcohol, and measures to mitigate those impacts such as measures to mitigate the negative effects of alcohol like drunk-driving and domestic violence
Fairness	• Anti-discrimination policies • Measures to ensure gender parity • Fair business practices with stakeholders such as suppliers
Respect	• Compliance • Respect culture and social norms of communities

It is interesting to note that organisations that have become poster cards of corporate governance failings also had core values. Enron's core values were communication, respect and integrity. The accounting fraud and other governance failures contradict the principle of integrity. Barclays Plc was at the heart of the LIBOR (London Inter Bank Offered Rate) scandal (fraudulent action relating to false increase or reduction of interbank rates) in 2012, but has core values that include respect, integrity, service, excellence and stewardship. Volkswagen's core values of responsibility and sustainability and the company's narrative around these core values, particularly responsibility to the economy, society and the environment, are not compatible with the emissions scandal of 2015. These examples raise questions about the value of values or why organisations behave in a manner that contradicts their core values. The next section explains unethical conduct and the drivers of unethical behaviour.

Unethical conduct in business

Having defined ethical business and seen practical examples of the application of the values of an organisation to doing business, let us now turn to unethical business practices.

Common forms of unethical business practices

Unethical business practices are wide ranging. Some make headlines while the majority do not. Simply put, these are practices that are contrary to our values. Table 8.3 lists some practices that have made headlines in the press in the recent past.

Table 8.3: Examples of unethical conduct

Sector	Unethical conduct
Banking	• Libor scandal • Wells Fargo fake accounts scandal
Pharmaceuticals	• Norvatis Korea executives charged with bribing doctors • GlaxoSmithKline bribery practices in China
Automobile industry	• Volkswagen emissions scandal
Technology	• Samsung heir corruption case • Tax avoidance
Clothing industry	• Child labour • Low wages • Health and safety issues
Sports	• Corruption (e.g. Fifa corruption scandal) • Match fixing

The other practices that are common in day-to-day business include transfer pricing, misleading product labels and tax evasion, and increasingly tax avoidance practices of multinational corporations, conflicts of interest, business practices that fuel conflict in resource-rich countries, and unsafe working conditions including sweatshops in the garment industry.

Some of the above practices exploit loopholes in legal and regulatory frameworks while others are illegal and orchestrated by organisations, often with the knowledge of senior executives.

Drivers of unethical conduct

There are several drivers of unethical conduct, including competition and the desire for short-term gains, performance-related pressures including investor expectations, technology and other smart moves that make people assume the practices will not be discovered. Volkswagen's manipulation of vehicle emissions was driven by commercial factors – the need to appeal to customers in the US market about 'low emissions' vehicles.

Some scholars attribute the prevalence of unethical conduct to technology and institutional failures (Mukerjee, 2016). On the other hand, some researchers have applied game theory analysis to the study of drivers of unethical conduct and found that even the most morally competent persons may disregard ethical considerations due to a phenomenon called ethical fading (Bazerman and Tenbrunsel, 2011; Tenbrunsel et al., 2012). In summary, Bazerman argues:

> Unethical conduct happens because people are unconsciously fooling themselves... that is why lapses in action in the corporate world seem so pervasive and intractable.

The above factors point to a problem of lack of a culture of ethics within organisations – that is, absence of a system that embeds the values of an organisation into the broad spectrum of the organisation's operations.

Consequences of unethical conduct

It might be possible to get away with unethical conduct and it is possible that there are more cases of unethical conduct that go unnoticed than those that are discovered. It is not about the 'smartest guys in the room' or the ability to get away with it. Unethical conduct has far-reaching implications for business. It is a breach of trust, undermines arm's-length transactions, damages reputation, and leads to loss of value and investments, among other things. The consequences far outweigh the short-term benefits.

Consequences for business

Unethical conduct:

- damages reputation and brand value. Leading brands such as Barclays and Volkswagen have had their brand reputation dented by the recent scandals;
- causes internal disruptions due to resignation of staff and senior leaders as well as investigations by regulators and in some cases, law enforcement agencies;
- diverts attention and resources from business activities to corrective action;
- causes loss of revenue, earnings and market share. For companies that are listed on stock exchanges, negative publicity that results from unethical conduct affects share price hence loss of value for investors. Consumer trust is dented, leading to low sales and revenue;
- causes loss of resources and assets due to bribery and corruption;
- breeds a culture of dishonesty and greed. Enron and the LIBOR scandals are good examples of this;
- results in low job satisfaction and productivity due to unfair and unethical practices; and
- damages brand value and goodwill.

Consequences for investors

Investor expectations may drive unethical conduct, so it is important for both organisations and investors to understand the consequences. A balanced approach to risk and return is required. As key corporate governance players, owners/founders/investors need to articulate their expectations clearly regarding ethical conduct as a measure to guard against loss of value resulting from falling share prices in the aftermath of unethical conduct, since increased costs of doing business as a result of corrective measures, loss of key business relationships and disruptions following discovery of unethical conduct may cause competitors to gain market share.

Consequences for individuals

The consequences for individuals include loss of jobs, damage to reputation, prosecution and conviction that results in conviction and/or payment of heavy penalties. The head of Volkswagen's US environment and engineering office was arrested on 7 January 2017 on charges related to the emissions scandal. The former CEO of Enron Jeff Skilling was convicted in 2006 and sentenced to 24 years' imprisonment for charges relating to Enron's accounting fraud. Samsung Group's Vice Chairman Lee was arrested in February 2017 on allegations of bribery and corruption.

Unethical conduct may be grounds for director disqualification. In addition, persons involved in unethical conduct may not meet the fit and proper criteria for appointment as directors in regulated entities. The criteria used by the Financial Conduct Authority (FCA) to assess fitness and propriety includes honest, integrity and reputation, among other factors.

Consequences for society

Unethical business practices can also lead to activities or practices that are harmful to society, including producing harmful or substandard goods, pollution and damage to the environment, among others. Unethical business practices can fuel conflict and various multinational corporations have been implicated in fuelling conflict in various parts of the world. Royal Dutch Shell was for several years implicated in environmental degradation and conflict in Nigeria. A 2010 report by *Corporate Watch* cited several British corporations involved in fuelling war in the Democratic Republic of Congo.

Governance, ethics and sustainability

The single most important lesson from corporate failures is that ethics is a core component of the governance of organisations. The historical focus on risk, controls, compliance and other aspects of governance has led to repeated cycles of failures and scandals and demonstrated a clear vacuum – ethics. Figure 8.1 demonstrates the importance of ethics to the entire governance framework.

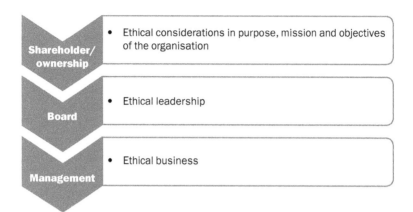

Figure 8.1: Ethical responsibilities of key governance players

Ethical leadership

Ethics must start with leadership. Ethical lapses at the leadership level have grave implications for governance. The UK Corporate Governance Code 2018 clearly states that the board should establish a company's purpose, strategy and values, and ensure that these are aligned with the company's culture. Directors should also embody and promote the desired culture of the company, setting the tone from the top.

The ethical leadership role of the board is unique and has three components. First, directors should be persons of integrity. Individual directors should be persons of integrity with no track record of unethical conduct. The International Organisation of Securities Commissions (IOSCO) provides guidance on assessment of the fitness and propriety of key persons which includes aspects of honesty, integrity, fairness and ethical behaviour. The following quote is an extract from the IOSCO assessment criteria. Key persons include directors, and although the criteria makes specific reference to key persons in the financial services industry, it is important to understand that fitness and propriety is relevant to all aspects of organisational leadership.

3.2 Honesty, integrity, fairness, ethical behavior

Key persons who are honest, diligent and independent-minded, who act ethically and with integrity and fairness are essential to the good reputation and trustworthiness of the financial services industry in general and of individual entities in particular. In determining the honesty, integrity and reputation of the applicant/key person, the Financial Regulator may consider among other things, whether the applicant/key person has been convicted, on indictment, of dishonesty, fraud, money laundering, theft or financial crime within the last 10 years. This may be regarded by the Financial Regulator as an indication that a person is not fit and proper and will, in principle, bar a person from holding a position as the Regulated Person. Where a person has a conviction dating beyond ten years, such information may be notified to the Financial Regulator. Older convictions or indictments will be reviewed by the Financial Regulator in order to adjudicate on the application

(IOSCO, 2009)

Second, directors are required to behave ethically. In the exercise of their duties and responsibilities, directors have an ongoing obligation to observe principles of ethics. Decision making should be guided by ethical principles and values such as independence, transparency and acting in the best interests of the company.

The third component relates to governance of ethics of the organisation. The board has the responsibility to ensure that the organisation has a code of ethics and that the organisation has effective processes for compliance with ethical values of the organisation.

The King IV Code of Corporate Governance for South Africa, 2016
In addition to setting the example with its own ethical behavior, the governing body should ensure that it governs the ethics of the organization. The critical role of ethics cannot be overstated. As King III put it 'ethics… *is the foundation of and reasons for corporate governance*.'

(King IV Code of Corporate Governance)

The key things to note are that the application of ethical standards and values must start with the leadership of the organisation. The leadership must demonstrate buy-in and commitment to ethical values and principles. The leadership must fulfil its ethical leadership responsibilities and provide clear direction on ethical matters.

The collective responsibility to demonstrate ethical leadership

The governing body as a collective must set the ethical example & tone…must be unified on matters such as the core purpose of the organisation, its culture, its drivers of value… key stakeholder groupings & their legitimate & reasonable needs, interests & expectations.

(King IV Code of Corporate Governance)

The King Code of South Africa requires collective responsibility of the board for ethical leadership. Unlike shareholder matters where decision-making at the AGM is by majority vote or by special resolution on key matters specifically prescribed by the Companies Act, decision making by the board is by a decision of the majority and all directors are bound by decisions of the majority. Therefore, it is interesting when a code requires a board to rally collectively around issues such as purpose and culture.

The King IV code focuses on decision making processes of the board as the key areas where ethical leadership should be demonstrated. These are:

- acting with independence of mind and in the best interests of the organisation. There are several threats to independence including affiliations and business relationships. The code requires full disclosure of conflicts of interests and effective measures to manage or avoid them;
- an inclusive approach to governance that takes into account the legitimate and reasonable needs, interests and expectations of all stakeholders;
- collective and individual competence of the directors;
- diligence and devotion of sufficient time to the affairs of the organisation;
- access to information and sufficient working knowledge of the organisation, its industry, economic and social environment to aid decision making; and
- honesty and integrity in taking risks for reward.

Codes of ethics and the governance framework

A code of ethics articulates the ethical values of the organisation and serves as the key reference point for ethical conduct. The code should inform other policies and procedures of the organisation. Corporate governance standards do not prescribe the form, content and format of codes of ethics. However, a code should generally cover:

- the guiding principles for ethical conduct such as honesty, integrity, compliance and acting in the best interests of the organisation;
- compliance requirements – compliance with relevant laws, regulations and policies among others;

- dealing with conflicts of interest;
- outside engagements such as directorships;
- dealing with related and connected persons;
- communications;
- corporate opportunities;
- insider trading;
- confidential information;
- fraud and protection of company assets;
- bribery and corruption;
- gifts and entertainment;
- discrimination and harassment; and
- relations with stakeholders such as customers and suppliers.

The development of a code of ethics should be guided by the following good practices. It should not just be a tick-box exercise but should cover all important aspects relating to an organisation's activities, implementation of the code, monitoring compliance and measures to report unethical conduct.

- It is the board's responsibility to ensure that the organisation has a code of ethics.
- Codes should clearly articulate an organisation's values.
- Demonstrate high-level buy-in, e.g. statement, signature or endorsement by the board chairman and CEO.
- Comprehensive principles covering all aspects of the organisation's activities.
- The development of the code should take into account the internal (operations) and external (suppliers, customers, community, regulations, etc.) context.
- The code should outline the duties and responsibilities of various parties such as the board, senior management and employees.
- The code should have a clear implementation and enforcement framework including awareness measures such as employee orientation, regular or periodic awareness, clear communication policy and clear monitoring and reporting mechanisms.
- Safety/protection measures for those who report unethical conduct such as including whistleblowers.

The implementation of a code of ethics involves various players. Each player must understand their roles and responsibilities, as indicated in Figure 8.2.

Figure 8.2: Ethical responsibilities of various players

Creating an ethical culture

Culture refers to a way of life or to the practices and beliefs of a group or society. The practices and beliefs are established by custom or practice over a long period of time; a single act or event does not constitute culture. Having a code of ethics or leadership that observes principles of ethical governance does not of itself create an ethical culture. Ethics must be embedded into all aspects of the organisation. The following quote explains what happens when there is disconnect between the values of an organisation and the manner in which it conducts business.

> The episode means that people in positions of authority at Volkswagen devised this scheme, that engineers knowingly signed off on code that would defeat the purpose of EPA and Clean Air Act regulations, and that the massive cheat was allowed to continue for seven years until it was finally detected. This can only happen in a company that is ethically corrupt from the inside out, rooted in an ethics-free, *the ends justify the means,* culture, and yet, before this, no one suspected that VW was more unethical than any other large company

(Ethics Alarms, 2015)

Defining ethical culture

The King IV Code of Corporate Governance provides that ethical and effective leadership should result in an ethical culture, sustainable performance and value creation, adequate and effective control by the governing body, and protecting and building trust in the organisation, its reputation and legitimacy.

So what is ethical culture? As with ethics, it might be difficult to establish a concise definition. On one hand ethical culture may be seen as an end product of a process and therefore, simply put, an 'ethical culture is the outcome of ethical behaviour'. This means there are several processes that contribute to that outcome. Figure 8.3 illustrates the various components of an ethical culture.

Figure 8.3: Components of an ethical culture

- **Ethical leadership,** as stated earlier, is provided by the board. Organisations can also provide ethical leadership within the industries or sectors in which they operate by choosing to do business in a manner that upholds key ethical values such as integrity, responsibility and fairness, among others. The John Lewis Partnership in the United Kingdom is an example of an organisation that provides leadership in a business model that combines commercial acumen and corporate conscience.

- **Organisational values** are the ethical principles that guide the entire operations of the organisation. The UK Corporate Governance Code 2018 places responsibility for setting the company's values and standards on the board. These should permeate through all aspects of the organisation's operations. As noted by the Chairman of the Financial Reporting Council, Sir Winfried Bischoff, 'The strategy to achieve a company's purpose should reflect the values and culture of the company and should not be developed in isolation. Boards should oversee both.'
- **Ethics codes and policies** are the tools that guide day-to-day activities or operations.
- **Rewards and sanctions** – organisations are required to ensure that remuneration, rewards and incentives are aligned to the company's ethical values. Reward schemes should not encourage unethical conduct. This is challenging because reward schemes and compensation arrangements are among the leading causes of unethical conduct hence the introduction of malus and clawback clauses in compensation contracts. Organisations should applaud and encourage ethical conduct, and ensure that there are measures to deter and penalise unethical conduct.

The King IV Code of Corporate Governance defines ethical culture as the governance of ethics and corporate citizenship. This is both inward and outward looking. The governance of ethics focuses on internal measures to create an ethics culture, while corporate citizenship is outward looking and considers how an ethical business behaves in society.

Creating an ethical culture is fairly easy for new or young organisations because they are starting with a clean slate. Such organisations have a chance to address all the components of an ethical culture without any resistance. The issue of concern for such organisations is making a false start, such as failing to address ethical issues at leadership level or ensuring that the leadership sets the tone at the outset. In addition, it is important to understand that creating an ethical culture is a long-term and ongoing process. For organisations that have existed for some time, the issue is either creating an ethical culture where previously this was lacking or plugging loopholes that have created opportunities for ethical or governance failures. Both involve changing behaviour, and it is difficult to change behaviour when people are used to a certain way of doing things. This may happen when unethical conduct is discovered and leaders as well as those implicated are forced out or resign on their own initiative. In such circumstances, various issues should be considered.

Resignation or exit of those implicated or those who take responsibility for ethical lapses presents an opportunity for the organisation in various ways. First, it is an opportunity to identify leaders that will take corrective action. Second, as part of measures to restore brand image and the confidence of stakeholders, the organisation must send clear signals that it is prepared to do all it takes to address the problems. In other words, it must demonstrate a commitment to the highest ethical standards.

It is always in the best interests of the organisation to own up to lapses and commit to taking corrective action as opposed to attempting to cover up and divert attention away from the issue. This may create other problems including criminal acts such as perjury or falsification of evidence. Former Tyco International Chief Executive Dennis L. Kozlowski was convicted in 2005 of falsifying business records, among other counts. In some cases, public perception has been that a cover-up is worse than the conduct that is the subject of the cover-up.

The leadership of the organisation should be cautious in the actions they take immediately after unethical conduct has been exposed. Any attempt to act on an uninformed basis or to defend those implicated only creates further damage for the organisation.

A person in charge of taking corrective action requires first and foremost the support of the leadership, particularly the board. It must give clear signals that it fully backs corrective measures and will not tolerate any lapses. Therefore, it is important for the board to agree collectively on corrective measures and monitor the implementation of those measures. The board must assure itself that all aspects of ethical governance are functional. In addition, the board must identify key risk areas and ensure that these are adequately monitored and reported to the board.

It is interesting to note from the Volkswagen 2016 Annual Report that following the 2015 emissions scandal, the organisation emerged as the world's bestselling auto-maker in 2016, having delivered 10.3 million vehicles with sales revenues of €217.3 billion and an operating profit of €7.1 billion. Volkswagen's Chairman of the Management Board attributes this to various factors, including the commitment to the long-term strategy of transforming the company into a globally leading provider of sustainable mobility.

The business case for an ethical culture

Unethical conduct produces short-term gains including increased revenues, profitability and market share. However, when discovered, the consequences and value lost are enormous. Enron and Arthur Andersen are classic examples of the devastating effects of unethical conduct. Arthur Andersen's revenues grew steadily from 1992 and peaked at close to $1 billion in 2001. During that period, it would have been difficult to imagine that unethical conduct was the greatest threat to the business. It is important for boards and organisations to focus on the long term and understand the business case for an ethical culture, as illustrated in Figure 8.4 and explained below.

Figure 8.4: The business case for an ethical culture

- **Brand value** – brand reputation is one of the most valuable assets of an organisation. An ethical culture protects the image and reputation of an organisation contributes to improved performance which enhances the brand of an organisation. Enron was a trusted brand in the energy sector and considered the most innovative company for several years prior to the scandal:
  … a business's most valuable asset is its good name, its brand and reputation… A company's brand reputational value has four basic elements: expectations, perceptions, business relationships and unique intellectual property assets.

  (*Forbes*, 2010)

- **Organisational resources and assets** – an ethical culture protects the resources and assets of an organisation. Unethical conduct promotes various practices such as bribery and corruption that cause leakages or outflow of resources. It also sends the wrong signals to employees and other stakeholders that may encourage wastage, dishonesty and fraud. Litigation and other expenses related to investigations, and taking corrective action to restore confidence, lead to further leakage of resources that would otherwise be used to further the objects of the organisation. According to its 2015 consolidated financial statements, Volkswagen reported a loss of €1.3 billion that was driven largely by a provision of about €16.2 billion for the diesel emissions scandal. The company provided detailed information about the emissions issue in the key events section of the financial statements and the amounts set aside to address the issue that include €7.8 billion for recalls and repurchases, and €7.0 billion for legal risks. Unfortunately, these costs are borne by the shareholder.

- **Focus** – unethical conduct may disrupt an organisation for various reasons including resignation or dismissal of its employees and leadership, criminal and other investigations that divert the attention of employees and senior leadership. The time and resources spent on rebuilding trust often disrupt business plans and divert attention away from key strategic plans. The group management report contained in the 2015 Annual Report of Volkswagen mentioned measures taken to respond to the emissions scandal, including internal and external investigations commissioned by the company and establishment of a special committee by the supervisory board to coordinate all activities relating to the emissions issue.

- **Organisational strategy** – unethical conduct is often driven by short-term interests. An ethical culture helps organisations to think beyond immediate or short-term challenges and focus on long-term strategies.
- **Employee satisfaction** – an ethical culture creates an environment that embodies some components that contribute to employee satisfaction such as fairness, transparency and trust. Employee satisfaction contributes to improved performance.
- **Shareholder value** – shareholders of organisations that have engaged in unethical conduct lose value through negative publicity, declining revenues and costs of rectifying the damage caused by unethical conduct.
- **The link between ethical culture and ethical leadership** – Unethical conduct raises questions about the leadership of an organisation and in particular whether they condone unethical practices or have simply failed to provide ethical leadership. The relationship between ethical culture and ethical leadership is like that of the chicken and egg. The board has the responsibility for putting in place the necessary building blocks for an ethical culture, and in turn an ethical culture ensures that the organisation has a firm foundation in the form of ethical leadership.

Chapter summary

- Ethics cannot be divorced from business conduct.
- Ethical failures have proved that legal and regulatory frameworks cannot prevent unethical conduct.
- Ethical failures have far-reaching impacts for organisations, financial markets and society.
- Creating an ethical culture is a process and not an event. It requires clarity of purpose, alignment on values, strategy and how these are integrated into the operations of the organisation.

9   Future trends in corporate governance

Introduction

This chapter considers future trends in corporate governance. It explores how corporate governance practices are being used to resolve some global common issues, such as executive pay, increased regulation, the impact of the millennial generation and the societal impact of organisational activities.

Future trends

As we saw in Chapter 2, there are three main corporate governance regimes which form the basis of corporate governance best practice. These are:

- the UK Corporate Governance framework;
- the OECD Corporate Governance Principles; and
- the King Reports from South Africa.

In Chapter 1 we saw that the three regimes represented three different approaches to corporate governance: shareholder value, stakeholder and inclusive stakeholder. In recent years, there has been a convergence in these approaches with the development in some countries, such as the UK, of a more enlightened shareholder value approach to governance which brings into the approach some stakeholder views. This convergence, it is argued has come about due to the emergence globally of some common issues which corporate governance seeks to resolve. This chapter explores those common issues.

Hybrid corporate governance systems

Flexibility in the application of corporate governance best practices is still important, so the maintenance of a voluntary regime rather than mandatory laws and regulations is still preferred in many countries. There is recognition that in lesser developed markets, voluntary systems may require the support of mandatory provisions, especially in 'public interest' organisations such as financial institutions to protect the public. As we saw in Chapter 1, many countries are adopting hybrid approaches to their adoption of corporate governance practices, some involving laws and mandatory regulations and others codes of best practice.

In the UK, the primary source of governance practices is by way of the 'comply and explain' regime in codes of best practice. These codes have in recent years been supplemented by laws and regulations. The UK approach can be contrasted with the US approach, which has been to adopt governance practices through law – such as the Sarbanes Oxley Act 2002.

In South Africa, there has been a move from 'comply and explain' to 'apply and explain'. The idea behind it is that it allows organisations to explain how they are applying the code and why, in a positive manner rather than in the perceived negative of explaining why they are not complying with a code and hoping investors agree.

Corporate governance for other sectors

Corporate governance laws, regulations, standards and codes are being developed for sectors in addition to listed companies. Historically, as we have seen, corporate governance codes and regulations were developed to protect shareholders in listed companies. Over the last 25 years, as corporate governance has spread, there has been a growing realisation that governance is relevant to all organisations, not just corporates. Different countries have dealt with how to apply governance to different types of organisations in different sectors in different ways. Some have developed 'umbrella' codes or principles of governance that apply to all organisations, such as the King Codes in South Africa. Others have created different codes for different types of organisations and for different sectors, such as the UK, which has, for example, the UK Charity Governance Code 2017.

Corporate governance standards based on size and societal impact

There is a growing belief that governance standards across all organisations should be based on their size and societal impact rather on their ownership structure. This view is reflected in the UK Government's Green Paper on Corporate Governance Reform, issued in November 2016. Currently, in many countries, the strictest corporate governance standards apply to listed companies and banks, even though many non-listed companies and state-owned enterprises are larger than many of the listed companies. It therefore seems appropriate that they should be governed by similar standards. In countries such as South Africa, the corporate governance code applies to all organisations, with specific laws and regulations in place for organisations in different sectors. Other countries appear to be following suit in extending a tougher corporate governance regime to a wider group of companies.

Limitations of corporate governance frameworks

There is a growing recognition that corporate governance frameworks in themselves cannot solve all of society's ills. These frameworks appear to reduce the incidence of bad behaviour by those that run organisations, but they cannot prevent such bad behaviours entirely. The human factor plays a part. It is surprising to many that it has taken so long for society to recognise that corporate governance frameworks like other laws, regulations and codes do not always eliminate the negatives of human nature. The UK Financial Reporting Council's (FRC) 2016 Report, 'Corporate Culture and the Role of Boards', noted that 'while legislation, regulation and codes influence individual and corporate behaviour, they do not ultimately control it'.

There is a growing realisation that getting the right 'culture' within organisations is vital in achieving good governance. Sir David Walker in his report, 'A Review of Corporate Governance in UK Banks and Financial Institutions', published in 2009, argued that both the character and culture of board members were important for an effective board.

In 2014, the UK FRC published a guidance document entitled 'FRC Guidance on Risk Management, Internal Control and Related Financial and Business Reporting'. Many see the guidance as creating a seismic shift in an organisation's approach to risk, as it links risk to culture when it states: 'The board's responsibility for the organisation's culture is essential to the way in which risk is considered and addressed within the organisation and with external stakeholders.'

In 2016, the UK Institute of Business Ethics published the report 'Culture by Committee, the Pros and Cons', which looked at how boards in the UK deal with culture in their organisations. There are a growing number of FTSE listed companies who are establishing separate board level committees dealing with corporate responsibility, ethics or sustainability. The report found 30 FTSE 100 and 15 FTSE 250 companies which had such committees. The main reason cited for such committees was the growing burden of non-financial risk. Audit committees are often seen to be overloaded and may not have the skills to consider non-financial matters, many of which carry the potential of huge reputational risk.

Licence to operate

Organisations appear to be realising that they are not 'islands' but have to earn a licence to operate within the communities within which they function. Identification of key stakeholders and the management of their interests and expectations have therefore been growing in importance for many organisations. Understanding one's stakeholders has become an important part of strategy development for many organisations.

Governments too have been considering what measures could be put in place to ensure that the connections between boards of directors and stakeholders are strengthened, especially those who have less power in the relationship but have a greater reliance on the organisation's performance for their own subsistence, among them employees and small businesses. In some quarters there is an expectation that larger companies, whether they are listed or not, should be expected to meet higher minimum standards of corporate governance and reporting due to the societal impact their decisions might have.

For countries to prosper economically, businesses of all sizes and individuals have to create value. To enable them to achieve this and for a country to create maximum value, there needs to be a framework in which people and organisations are able to succeed and prosper. All stakeholders need to have trust and confidence in this framework for it to be sustainable.

Reach of laws, regulations, standards and codes

Many countries are applying the laws, regulations, standards and codes of the parent company in their jurisdiction to all of the companies within the 'group' wherever they are in the world. Examples of this are the US Foreign Corrupt Practices Act and the UK Bribery Act 2010. Another example is the EU General Data Protection Regulation (GDPR) which applies to all companies, wherever they are located, that process or hold the personal data of EU citizens. Companies selling goods and services to EU countries will therefore be caught by this regulation.

Climate change

Governance is being seen by many as a response to the issues of climate change and the ever-increasing scarcity of resources. There is a growing recognition around the world that the focus on financial capital alone will not bring success in an organisation. This is being led by the 'millennial generation', those born since 1984, who are currently the largest generational group. Their views and opinions are starting to set the global agenda and it appears that they are more concerned about the planet than financial issues. Other capitals such as human, intellectual, natural and social are therefore often more important to them than financial capital. The focus of prior generations has been financial capital, as reflected in the plethora of financial reporting required of organisations.

> **KING IV REPORT ON CORPORATE GOVERNANCE FOR SOUTH AFRICA 2016 STATES OF THE MILLENNIAL GENERATION (MILLENNIALS)**
> Their concerns are beginning to set the global agenda. Millennials have shown that they are concerned about the global environment crunch much more than the global financial crisis. They are consequently attracted to companies who have integrated the six capitals into their business models. (The six capitals, set out in the International Integrated Reporting Council's Integrated Reporting [Framework are financial, manufactured, human, intellectual, natural, and social and relationship capital.)

The recent introduction in many organisations of 'integrated thinking' reflects this shift in importance of non-financial capitals. The International Integrated Reporting Council defines integrated thinking as 'the active consideration by an organisation of the relationships between its various operating and functional units and capitals that the organisation uses or affects'. Organisations should use integrated thinking when developing strategies to ensure that all the resources they utilise within their operations are used effectively, leading to a reduction in costs and a maximisation of performance for the organisation. This concept is also referred to as inclusive capitalism.

Focus on sustainability

There is a growing focus, especially in developing countries, on corporate governance as a mechanism for ensuring sustainability of organisations. Human rights-based approaches to development reflect similar concepts and principles of governance, transparency, accountability and responsibility through empowerment and ethical considerations which are all deemed important for economic sustainability. Even in developed countries, the focus is on more long-term approaches to the utilisation of capital to create sustainable value rather than the previous short-term view, which many believe led to the 2008 financial crisis.

Millennial generation's approach to confidentiality

The fundamental change in the world's view to 'transparency' caused by social media and the internet which has been reflected in the high-profile 'leaks' of information at all levels of society, the most well-known one being Wikileaks. The millennial generation's approach to confidentiality is very different to that of prior generations. Older generations treat privacy and confidentiality as the same. You can share something that is private and assume if you say so that it will be kept confidential. Millennials tend to see them as two different things. Is something is private you keep it to yourself, i.e. confidential. If you share it with anyone then it is out there, i.e. no longer confidential. The expectation is that it will be shared on the internet. Older generations are often appalled when a perceived private moment is recorded and then released onto the internet. It is seen as an invasion of privacy. Millennials frequently assume that everything they do when they are not alone is being shared, i.e. is public. The only way to keep something private is not to share it. Corporates, like governments, are waking up to this fact and are having to redesign policies, processes and procedures to deal with this issue.

Mandatory reporting requirements for non-financial information

The introduction in many countries of mandatory reporting requirements for non-financial information – for example, the UK's Strategic Report, the European's directive on environmental, social and governance reporting, the US SEC's reporting requirements and the growing requirements in many countries for listed companies. KPMG's tri-annual 'Survey of Corporate Responsibility Reporting 2015' cited legislation as the primary driver for corporate responsibility reporting. This reflected the increased regulatory reporting requirements globally. Previous KPMG surveys, when corporate responsibility reporting was mainly voluntary, cited business reasons as the driver for corporate responsibility reporting, among them reputation, brand, ethical considerations, innovation and learning, employee motivation and risk mitigation.

Emergence of technology governance

Globally, there is an ever greater reliance on technology. Organisations are required to manage the risks associated with technological disruptions within their organisations as well as an often 'insatiable' desire by management in many organisations to keep up with the latest technological developments. This requires governance. The King III Corporate Governance Code, in South Africa, was one of the first to recognise the importance of 'technology governance' in 2009. King IV has developed this further.

There is a growing recognition that cybersecurity should be high in the board's agenda. Recent global cyberattacks have highlighted the importance of cybersecurity risk management for board directors. Companies no longer have a choice as to whether they mitigate against cyberattacks. In future, this should be an important part of their risk management process. Countries are starting to look at whether they need to regulate with respect to cybersecurity. For example, the US Securities and Exchange Commission has expanded its focus on cybersecurity already taking action against corporations for not protecting customer data against cyberattacks.

Governance of risk

Previously, risk was seen primarily as a management function for financial institutions. Despite corporate governance codes talking about the board's responsibility for risk as far back as the early 1990s, many boards delegated this responsibility. Today, boards in all types of organisations and sectors are taking risk management more seriously.

THE UK FRC'S GUIDANCE ON RISK MANAGEMENT, INTERNAL CONTROL AND RELATED FINANCIAL AND BUSINESS REPORTING STATES:

The Board has responsibility for an organisation's overall approach to risk management and internal control. The Board's responsibilities are:

- Ensuring the design and implementation of appropriate risk management and internal control systems that identify the risks facing the company and enable the board to make a robust assessment of the principal risks;
- Determining the nature and extent of principal risks faced and those risks which the organisation is willing to take in achieving its strategic direction (determining its risk appetite);
- Ensuring that appropriate culture and reward systems have been embedded throughout the organisation;
- Agreeing how the principle risks should be managed or mitigated to reduce the likelihood of their incidence or their impact;
- Monitoring and reviewing the risk management and internal control systems, and the management's process of monitoring and reviewing, and satisfying itself that they are functioning effectively and that corrective action is being taken where necessary; and
- Ensuring sound internal and external information and communication processes and taking responsibility for external communication on risk management and internal control.

Governance of information

The governance of information is also becoming critical for organisations. The management of both information and knowledge can offer competitive advantage, and many organisations are increasing their focus on both areas. Governing bodies are increasing being expected to ensure that information and knowledge are managed effectively within their organisations and that they are protected.

Gender diversity

It is increasingly recognised that diversity is key for a successful organisation and introducing more women at leadership level introduces broader perspectives and new ways to manage problems. It also allows organisations across all three sectors (private, public and not-for-profit) to tap into the entire talent pool rather than deprive themselves of half of it. McKinsey has conducted global research which shows that organisations with a greater share of women on their boards of directors and executive committees tend to perform better financially.

The numbers of women on boards are increasing either through a system of quotas or the 'comply and explain' approach. Propelled by Norway, which in two years set and achieved a 40% quota for women directors for all listed companies, other countries have instituted mandates so that currently 23 countries have quotas for listed and state-owned companies. According to the latest research from the International Business Report by Grant Thornton, globally, 47% of senior managers, both men and women, are now in favour of having quotas for women on the boards of large listed companies.

Some countries have adopted an approach in which the government regulators provide guidance on what they consider good policy and practices and ask companies either to comply or to disclose publicly why they did not. In 2011, in the UK, Lord Davies, chair of the Review of Women on Boards, set a target of 25% of women on boards of UK listed companies in the FTSE 100 and used disclosure requirements to achieve that target in 2015. IN 2015, Hampton-Alexander set a new target of women on boards at 33% by 2020.

Other diversity issues

In addition to women on boards, other aspects of diversity are being considered in many countries whether this is more employee representation on boards, more ethnically diverse board members and a wider age spread. What appears to be important in constituting a board is achieving the diversity appropriate for the organisation. If the organisation is aimed at a young diverse market, then the board should reflect in some part that market.

Executive pay

In many developed countries the focus of corporate governance in recent years seems to be polarised around the issue of executive pay. This seems due to continue as there is a widespread perception that executive pay has become increasingly disconnected from the pay of the employees who work for them and also that it is no longer in line with the underlying long-term performance of companies.

As we saw in Chapter 2, many countries require a part of executive pay to be based on the performance of the organisation. How performance is measured depends on each organisation and may be based on measures such as total shareholder return (TSR) or on the economic value created by the organisation. One challenge has been that these measurement criteria have often led to opaque executive pay packages, with the executives themselves often being unclear regarding what level of pay they receive for what performance.

The ongoing debate is around what level of approval shareholders should exercise on executive pay. In the UK, shareholders of listed companies, since 2013, have a binding vote on pay policies at least once every three years and an annual advisory vote on actual pay awards made to directors under the shareholder-approved pay policies. The EU Shareholder Rights Directive amendments will bring this requirement in across the EU in 2019.

Organisations are required in most countries to make disclosures on executive pay. These disclosures can be on an aggregate or individual basis. Evidence seems to suggest that disclosure may have had the opposite effect to that intended when first introduced in many countries, in that it may have led to an increase in executive pay. Transparency in pay has led to both executives and remuneration consultants being able to make comparisons across companies. As each company strives to stay within a predefined salary bracket (for example, top 25th percentile), pay is ratcheted up. The Manifest Pay and Performance Survey 2015 concluded that total pay for UK CEOs of the FTSE 100 companies had quadrupled over the last 18 years.

THE G20/OECD CORPORATE GOVERNANCE PRINCIPLES 2015 CALL FOR:
the disclosure of remuneration of board members and key executives. In particular, it is important for shareholders to know the remuneration policy as well as the total value of compensation arrangements made pursuant to this policy. Shareholders also have an interest in how remuneration and company performance are linked when they assess the capability of the board and the qualities they should seek in nominees for the board. The different forms of say-on-pay (binding or advisory vote, ex-ante and/or ex post, board members and/or key executives covered, individual and/or aggregate compensation, compensation policy and/or actual remuneration) play an important role

---

in conveying the strength and tone of shareholder sentiment to the board. In the case of equity-based schemes, their potential to dilute shareholders' capital and to powerfully determine managerial incentives means that they should be approved by shareholders, either for individuals or for the policy of the scheme as a whole. Shareholder approval should also be required for any material changes to existing schemes.

Excessive pay

There is a growing recognition that excessive pay is not just an issue for listed company executives. Many countries suffer from income inequality. This is not something corporates can fix alone, but an issue for governments. In fact, in many countries, corporate executives are a relatively small proportion of the highly paid individuals in a country, with celebrities and sports stars often being paid considerably more.

Tax 'blacklisting'

In recent years many companies, among them Apple, Amazon, IKEA, Google and Starbucks, have come under attack for their tax planning. This has led to discussions at the G20 about how some of these 'legal' tax planning practices can be managed by governments. The disclosure of the Panama Papers in 2015 has also highlighted that the issue is broader than just companies, with many high-profile individuals being found to be involved in forms of 'legal' tax planning. One response to this phenomenon has been the EU blacklisting of countries seen to be offering services and products to assist people and companies avoid paying tax in their countries of origin. Boards should be discussing the reputational and other risks around tax practices affecting their companies.

Pension protection

Many countries are focusing their attention on ensuring that their populations provide for their retirement. Pension liberalisation is becoming common in developing countries, allowing non-state organisations to offer pension products. Experience in the UK, from Robert Maxwell in the early 1990s to Carillion in 2018, has shown that corporate pensions are affected when organisations fail. In January 2018,

Theresa May, the UK Prime Minister, stated in the *Observer* that the UK government would be considering bringing into law further pension protection following the lessons learned from the failure of Carillion.

Sexual harassment in the workplace

The recent high-profile cases of sexual harassment emerging across all industries and sectors present organisations globally with real reputational risk. Boards should ensure that policies and guidelines on sexual harassment in the workplace are established and are fit for purpose.

Pay equality

The issue of pay equality between men and women has again been highlighted, with high-profile cases such as the pay practices of the BBC in 2017. Again this poses a reputational risk for many organisations. Boards should be reviewing their pay policies and ensuring that their remuneration practices are fair. There have been examples where employees have taken their own decision to ensure equality in pay between genders. In January 2018, Johan Lundgren, the new easyJet CEO, offered to have his salary cut to the same level as his female predecessor, Dame Carolyn McCall, when the airline revealed its female staff were paid about half the rate of men on average.

Importance of governance professionals

The importance of having a governance professional within an organisation is also growing around the globe. Traditionally, in common law countries, the role of the company secretary is well known and respected as an important position in a governance framework. In more and more civil law countries, the position of the company or corporate secretary is being included as an important provision in corporate governance regulations. Within non-corporates, a similar position is being created or the responsibilities of the company secretary are being given to an individual within the organisation. It is hoped through the current debates on corporate governance in the UK that the position of the company secretary in larger private companies and those with a societal impact will be reinstated. More information on the role of the company secretary can be found in Chapter 4.

UK Stewardship Code

During 2018, the FRC expects to publish a detailed consultation on changes to the UK Stewardship Code. An initial consultation on format and content of the Code was published as part of the FRC's Consultation for the 2018 UK Corporate Governance Code in December 2017.

Brexit

The impact of the UK leaving the EU on the governance and performance of organisations either resident in the UK or elsewhere is yet to be established. It is recognised, however, that there will be an impact and boards should be monitoring and planning for what this may be.

Chapter summary

- Future trends in corporate governance have now become global and this has led to a convergence in approaches to corporate governance.
- New issues such as the impact of millennials in the workplace and cybersecurity are challenging boards to develop new governance practices and strategies to ensure continued performance and sustainability of their organisations.
- The future promises some interesting times ahead in the field of corporate governance.

References

African Peer Review Mechanism (APRM) Reports about good governance. www.aprm-au.org

Albani, Marco and Henderson, Kimberly (2004), *Creating Partnerships for Sustainability*, McKinsey, July.

Bartels, Wim (KPMG Netherlands) and King, Adrian (KPMG Australia) (2015), *Survey of Corporate Responsibility Reporting*, KPMG.

Bazerman, Max H. and Tenbrunsel, Ann E. (2011), *Bling Spots: Why We Fail to Do What's Right and What to Do about It*, Princeton, NJ: Princeton University Press.

Bernstein, Ann (2010), *The Case for Business in Developing Countries*, Penguin Books.

Brigham, Alexander F. and Linssen, Stefan (2010), 'Your brand reputational value is irreplaceable. Protect it', *Forbes*, January. www.forbes.com/2010/02/01/brand-reputation-value-leadership-managing-ethisphere.html (accessed 8 March 2017).

Browne, John and Nuttall, Robin (2013), *Beyond CSR: Integrated External Engagement*, McKinsey, March.

Browne, John and Nuttall, Robin (2013), *How Companies Succeed by Engaging Radically with Society*, Ebury Publishing.

Cadbury, Adrian (1992), *Report of the Committee on Financial Aspects of Governance*, GEE.

Clerc, Christophe (2007), *Proportionality between Ownership and Control in EU Listed Companies: Comparative Legal Study*, Sheerman and Sterling LLP.

Cone Communications (2015), *Millennial CSR Study*, Cone Communications.

Deloitte (n.d.), 'The changing role of the company secretary'. www2.deloitte.com/ie/en/pages/legal/articles/changing-role-secretary.html (accessed 22 February 2017).

Eccles, Robert G. and Krzus, Michael P. (2010), *One Report: Integrated Reporting for Sustainable Strategy*, John Wiley & Sons, Inc.

Ekatah, Innocent, Samy, Martin, Bampton, Robert and Halabi, Abdel (2011), 'The relationship between corporate social responsibility and profitability: the case of Royal Dutch Shell PLC', *Corporate Reputation Review*.

Esty, Daniel C. and Winston, Andrew S. (2006, 2009), *Green to Gold*, John Wiley & Sons, Inc.

Ethics Alarms (2015), 'The VW scandal: huge consequences, simple ethics lessons, ominous implications' (9). https://ethicsalarms.com/2015/09/27/the-vw-scandal-huge-consequences-simple-ethics-lessons-ominous-implications (accessed 28 February 2017).

Ferran, Eilis (2008), *Principles of Corporate Finance Law*, Oxford: Oxford University Press, p. 9.

Friedman, Milton (1962), *Capitalism and Freedom*, University of Chicago.

Friedman, Milton (1970), 'The social responsibility of business to increase its profits', *New York Times*, 13 September.

G20/OECD (2015), *Principles of Corporate Governance*.

G20/OECD (2015), *Report to G20 Finance Ministers and Central Bank Governors*, September.

Global Corporate Governance Forum (2009), *Stakeholder Engagement and the Board: Integrating Governance Practices*, August.

Globalreporting.com (n.d.), www.globalreporting.com.

ICSA (2017), *The Governance Institute and Recruitment Specialist: The Core Partnership*, ICSA, April.

Institutional Voting Information Service (IVIS) (n.d.), Examples of corporate governance guidelines. www.ivis.co.uk.

International Corporate Governance Network (ICGN) (2014), *ICGN Global Governance Principles*, ICGN.

International Finance Corporation (Part of the World Bank Group) Publications. www.ifc.org/corporate governance

International Organisation of Securities Commissions (IOSCO) (2009), *IOSCO Fit and Proper Assessment: Best Practice Final Report*.

Investment Management Association (n.d.), *Asset Management Survey*.

Johnson, G., Scholes, K. and Whittington, R. (2008), *Exploring Corporate Strategy* (8th ed.), London: Prentice Hall.

Kaplan, Robert S. and Norton, David P. (n.d.), *Using a Balanced Scorecard as a Strategic Management System*, Boston, MA: Harvard Business School Press.

Keys, Tracey, Malinight, Thomas and Graaf, Kees van der (2009), *Making the Most of Corporate Responsibility*, McKinsey, December.

King and Woods Mallesons, (2016), 'Take action! An update on shareholder activism', April.

Klapper, Leora F. and Love, Inessa (2002), *Corporate Governance, Investor Protection and Performance in Emerging Markets*. World Bank Policy Working Paper No. 2818.

KPMG (n.d.), Global surveys on why organizations carry out and report CSR activities.

Lagerberg, Francesca (n.d.), *Women in Business: The Value of Diversity*, Grant Thornton.

Larcker, David F. and Tayan, Brian (2016), *Chairman and CEO: The Controversy over Board Leadership Structure. Stanford Closer Look Series* (June).

Larkin, Judy (2002), *Strategic Reputation Risk Management*, Palgrave MacMillan.

Lee, Joseph (n.d.), 'From "house keeping" to "gatekeeping": the enhanced role of the company secretary in the governance system'. https://papers.ssrn.com/sol3/papers.cfm?abstract_id=2733180 (accessed 17 March 2017).

Montagnon, Peter (2016), *Culture by Committee, the Pros and Cons*, Institute of Business Ethics, ICSA & MAZARS.

Miller, Robert (2010), 'The vile scramble for loot: how British corporations are fueling war in the DR Congo', *Corporate Watch* (9). https://corporatewatch.org/content/april-09-2010-vile-scramble-loot-how-british-corporations-are-fuelling-war-dr-congo.

MM&K (2015), *Manifest Pay and Performance Survey*, MM&K.

Mukherjee, Amit S. (2016), 'Why we're seeing so many corporate scandals', *Harvard Business Review*, December. https://hbr.org/2016/12/why-were-seeing-so-many-corporate-scandals (accessed 28 February 2017).

Ogoola, Justice James Munange (2014), 'Ethics: the heart and soul of the legal profession', in Dennision, D. Brian and Kalyegira, Pamela Pibihikara (eds), *Legal Ethics and Professionalism Handbook for Uganda: Global Ethics and African Law*, pp. 29–30.

Ottaway, Joanne (2011), 'Improving auditor independence in Australia: is mandatory audit firm rotation the best opinion?', Melbourne Law School, December.

Porter (n.d.), Theoretical debate on 'doing well by doing good'.

Post, J.E., Preston, L.D. and Sachs, S. (2002), *Refining the Corporation: Stakeholder Management and Organizational Wealth*, Stanford, CA: Stanford Business Books.

Sarbanes, Paul and Oxley, Michael G. (2002), The Sarbanes Oxley Act.

Sheerman and Sterling LLP (2007), *Proportionality between Ownership and Control in EU Listed Companies: Comparative Legal Study*. www.ecgi.org/osov/documents/study_report_en.pdf (accessed 3 May 2017).

Stergiou, Versiliki (2011), *The Complex Relationship of Concentrated Ownership Structures and Corporate Governance*, p.147. Thesis submitted to the Department of Law at the London School of Economics and Political Science. http://etheses.lse.ac.uk/464/1/ Stergiou_The%20complex%20relationship%20of%20concentrated%20ownership.pdf (accessed May 3 2017).

Tenbrunsel, Ann E., Drekmann, Kristin A., Wade Bensoni, Kimberly A. and Bazerman, Max H. (2007), *The Ethical Mirage: A Temporal Explanation as to Why We Aren't as We Think We Are*, Harvard Business School. www.hbs.edu/faculty/Publication%20Files/08-012. pdf (accessed 23 May 2017).

The Economist (2012), 'The Rotten Heart of Finance: a scandal over key interest rates is about to go global' (7). www.economist.com/ node/21558281 (accessed 28 April 2017).

Tricker, Bob (1984), *Corporate Governance and Business Ethics*, Oxford: Oxford University Press.

UK Financial Reporting Council (2014), *FRC Guidance on Risk Management, Internal Control and Related Financial and Business Reporting*, FRC, September.

UK Financial Reporting Council (2016), *Corporate Culture and the Role of the Board*, FRC.

U.S. Government Printing Office (1985), *U.S. President's Commission on Industrial Competitiveness*, Washington, March.

Vermulen, Erik P.M. (2005), 'The role of the law in developing efficient corporate governance frameworks, in *Corporate Governance of Non-Listed Companies in Emerging Markets*, OECD, pp. 91–130.

Walker, Sir David (2009), *Review of Corporate Governance in UK Banks and Financial Institutions*, British Banker Association, Printers Hall.

Walton, Elise (2011), 'Chairmanship – the effective chair–CEO relationship', *Insight from the Board Room. Millstein Center for Corporate Governance and Performance*, working paper.

Werner, Charlotte, Devileard, Saudrine and Saucier Sultan, Sandra (2014), *Moving Women on the Top* (survey results), McKinsey Global, October.

Wiersema, Margareth and Mors, Marie Louise (2016), 'What board directors really think of gender quotas', *Harvard Business Review*, November. https://hbr.org/2016/11/what-board-directors-really-think-of-gender-quotas (accessed 15 May 2017).

Glossary

Accountability The requirement for a person or body in a position of responsibility to justify, explain or account for the exercise of authority given to him/her/it and performance or actions taken with that authority. Accountability is to the person or body from whom the authority is derived.

Board committee A committee established by the board of directors, with delegated responsibility for a particular aspect of the board affairs. For example, audit committee, remuneration committee and nomination committee.

Board evaluation The evaluation of the board, board committees, chairman and other individual directors carried out by companies typically every three years.

Box ticking approach An approach to compliance based on following all the specific rules or provisions in a code and not considering the principles that should be applied and circumstances where the principles are best applied by not following the detailed provisions.

Clawback The act of recovering sums paid, or withholding payment to directors or senior executives where there has been deemed to be deliberate disclosure of misleading information to increase entitlement to bonuses.

Corporate social responsibility (CRS) Responsibility shown by a company (or other organisations) for matters of general concern to the society in which it operates, such as protection of the environment, health and safety and social welfare.

Fairness Impartiality, lack of bias. In a corporate governance context, the quality of fairness refers to things that are done or decided in a reasonable manner, and with a sense of justice, avoiding bias typically to an organisation's stakeholders

Financial statement A statement issued annually by a company as part of its annual report containing financial information about the organisation. It usually comprises the balance sheet, profit and loss account, a cash flow statement, a statement of changes in equity and financial notes.

Institutional investor An organization or institution that invests funds of clients, savers or depositors. The main institutional investors in the UK are pension funds, insurance/life assurance companies, investment trust companies and mutual organizations such as unit trusts.

Integrated reporting Reporting on all aspects of the company's activities, financial and non-financial, that have relevance to the creation or loss of value in six areas of capital: financial, manufactured, human, intellectual property, natural and social.

Internal control A mechanism that is put in place to prevent an internal control risk (preventative control), reduce the potential impact of such a risk (corrective control), or detect a failure of internal control when it occurs (and initiate remedial action (detective control)).

Majority shareholder A shareholder holding a majority of the equity shares in company and so having a controlling interest in the voting power to remove directors from the board and so can control the board

Market manipulation This occurs when an individual distorts a market in the investments, creates a false or misleading impression of the value or price of an investment, or misuses relevant information before it is published. Although it is similar to insider dealing, which is a criminal offence, this is a civil offence under the Financial Services and Markets Act.

Millennials People born between 1982 and 2004 are generally known as millennials.

Reputational risk The risk to the reputation of a company of other organization in the mind of the public (including customers and suppliers) when a particular matter becomes public knowledge

Responsibility Having power and authority over something. A person in a position of responsibility should be held accountable for the exercise of that authority

Risk Management A process whereby an organisation identifies, assesses, mitigates and monitors risk within and organisation and reports on the effectiveness of the risk management systems to stakeholders.

Senior independent director An independent non-executive director who is the nominal head of all the non-executive directors (NEDs) on the board. The SID may act as a channel of communication between the

NEDS and the chairman, or, when necessary between major share-holders and the board.

Shareholder activism Refers to the active dialogue between shareholders and the boards of companies, to influence decisions by the board. An example is institutional investors voting, or threatening to vote, against the board of directors at general meetings.

Socially responsible investment Investing with due consideration for environmental, social and governance issues, because these can affect the value of the business. Also referred to as responsible investment.

Stakeholders An individual or group of individuals who have an interest in the organisation. Examples of stakeholders are shareholders, the directors, employees, customers, suppliers, the general public and the government.

Sustainability Conducting business operations for the long-term, for example, without using natural resources at such a rate or creating such environmental damage that continuation of the business will eventually become impossible.

Transparency Being open and clear about how you do business, whether this is in disclosure of information or the processes you adopt, for say, procurement and recruitment.

Index

Lightning Source UK Ltd.
Milton Keynes UK
UKHW021454040219
336727UK00005B/272/P